HOW MY GRANDFATHER STOLE A SHOE
AND SURVIVED THE HOLOCAUST IN UKRAINE

HOW MY GRANDFATHER STOLE A SHOE
AND SURVIVED THE HOLOCAUST IN UKRAINE

JULIE MASIS

Art by
Felix Lembersky

CHERRY ORCHARD BOOKS
2025

Library of Congress Cataloging-in-Publication Data

Names: Masis, Julie, 1981- author. | Lembersky, Felix, 1913-1970, illustrator.
Title: How my grandfather stole a shoe (and survived the Holocaust in Ukraine) / Julie Masis ; illustrated by Felix Lembersky.
Description: Boston : Cherry Orchard Books, an imprint of Academic Studies Press, 2025.
Identifiers: LCCN 2024047987 (print) | LCCN 2024047988 (ebook) | ISBN 9798887197098 (hardback) | ISBN 9798887197104 (paperback) | ISBN 9798887197111 (pdf) | ISBN 9798887197128 (epub)
Subjects: LCSH: Masis, Shlomo, 1913-2019. | Masis, Shlomo, 1913-2019--Family. | Holocaust, Jewish (1939-1945)--Ukraine--Transnistria (Territory under German and Romanian occupation, 1941-1944)--Biography. | Obodivka Ghetto (Obodivka, Ukraine)--Social conditions. | Holocaust, Jewish (1939-1945)--Moldova--Zguriţa. | Holocaust survivors--Massachusetts--Biography. | Masis, Julie, 1981---Travel--Europe, Eastern. | Masis family. | Jews--Moldova--Zguriţa--Social conditions. | Zguriţa (Moldova)--Biography.
Classification: LCC DS135.M64 M35 2025 (print) | LCC DS135.M64 (ebook) | DDC 940.53/18092 [B]--dc23/eng/20241220
LC record available at https://lccn.loc.gov/2024047987
LC ebook record available at https://lccn.loc.gov/2024047988

Copyright © Julie Masis, 2025

ISBN 9798887197098 (hardback)
ISBN 9798887197104 (paperback)
ISBN 9798887197111 (Adobe PDF)
ISBN 9798887197128 (ePub)

Book design by Julie Masis. Illustrations by Felix Lembersky, reproduced by permission.
Cover design by Julie Masis and Ivan Grave

Published by Cherry Orchard Books, and imprint of Academic Studies Press
1007 Chestnut Street
Newton, MA 02464, USA
press@academicstudiespress.com
www.academicstudiespress.com

For Dina and Alexander Masis.
For Eli Masis, and for everyone who will come after.

Contents

One Hundred Candles	1
Introduction	3
GRANDPA	**8**
How the War Started	9
The Rug that Hung on the Wall	12
Thrown Out of a Moving Train	14
The Zguritsa Pogrom	16
The Fruit Trees that Grew Along the Roads	18
How My Grandfather Stole a Shoe	19
The Bird that Wanted to Be Free	21
How the Youngest Brother Died	23
The Airport and the Hospital	25
The Selection	28
Villages at Dusk	30
The Frozen Bodies	32
The Nazi Who Rode a Motorcycle	34
Why Did Haim Come Back?	36
The Unlucky Wedding	39
Barefoot in the Snow	41
Grandpa Wants to Go Outside	44
Two Buckets of Potatoes and a Broken Bottle	46
If They Didn't Have Bread, They Gave Potatoes	49
Adam and Eve	51

How Grandpa Saved His Brother	53
Forced Labor	55
How Curiosity Saved Grandpa	57
The Collective Farm	59
Not Like Schindler	61
How I Wore Grandpa's Sweatpants	63
The Partisans Who Dressed as Nazis	65
The Soldiers With Feathers	67
Never Too Old to Dance	69
How Grandpa Milled Grain	71
Have a Good Year	73

GRANDMA — 75

From Romania to The Soviet Union	76
The Ticket to America	78
The Uncle Who Sold Bagels	80
Ten Years for Telling a Joke	82
The Truck That Came Too Late	84
Expelled From Soroca	86
Vertujani	88
The Frostbitten Feet	90
The German Wallet	92
A Conversation	94
The Stolen Bread	95
The Fake Email	97
Retaliation	98
An Unexpected Meeting	100
A Love Story in the Ghetto?	102
Did Grandpa Know?	104

The Red Cross	106
How Tsilia Met Shlomo	108
The Couple That Got Married in the Ghetto	110
How the Ghetto Was Liberated	112
Romania's Responsibility	114
How My Grandparents Got Married	116
How Grandpa Got His Suit Back	118
The Bag That Took the Train	120
How Grandpa Killed Two Nazis	122
How the War Ended	124
The Drive Home	127

GRANDDAUGHTER 129

How I Was Named	130
"Keep Moving, You Are Not a Tree!"	131
On the Road to Moldova	134
A Visit to Zguritsa	139
Zguritsa Before the War	142
The Cow in the Cemetery	144
The Roma Capital of the World	146
The Trip to Obodovka	149
A Classmate	156
The Righteous Among the Nations	158
Back in Odessa	160
Kyiv, the Capital of Ukraine	162
The Synagogue of Orhei	165
Chisinau in the Summer	167

AFTER THE WAR	**169**
The Famine of 1947	170
How a Poor Man Visited a Rich Man	172
Potato Diplomacy	174
The Free Cookies	176
Without His Grandparents	178
How the Horse Died	180
Yahrzeit	182
Childhood Games	184
The Blue Suit	186
Showing Disrespect	189
The Horse-Pulled Sleigh	190
Antisemitism	192
The Man who Wanted to Make My Father Blind	194
The Only Man in Zguritsa Who Had a Car	196
How a Tobacco Factory Cured Grandpa	199
The Antenna	201
The Most Important Thing in Life	204
The Matchmaker	207
Grandma's Letters	209
How My Father Got Arrested in the Cinema	211
How My Father Sent Butter in the Mail	214
The Hospital on the Way to America	216
How We Came to America	219
How Grandpa Got Lost	221
Grandpa's Trip to Israel	223
Why Grandpa Didn't Learn to Drive	224
Why Grandpa Didn't Remarry	225
Grandpa's Sunglasses	226

The Upcoming Birthday	228
How to Communicate Without Words	229
The Interview	230
One Hundred and a Half	232
Language	234
Grandpa's Lost Address Book	236
Ancestors at a Dinner Party	238
Acknowledgements	242

One Hundred Candles

In the photo that someone took that day, everyone is looking at the giant birthday cake, on which one hundred candles are burning. Everyone is hypnotized by the cake except for the birthday man, my grandpa Shlomo. He is standing at the center of the table right in front of the cake, but his eyes are focused on his great-grandson Joshik, who is just barely tall enough to see above the table. Joshik doesn't see grandpa. He sees only the cake with one hundred candles.

When the candles were blown out—someone must have said, "On the count of three, let's all take a deep breath and blow out the candles together!"—my father told everyone to take one candle from grandpa's cake as a good luck charm.

"Everyone who takes a candle from grandpa's cake will also live to one hundred," he announced.

I don't know how my father came up with this idea, but there were more candles on the cake than guests at the party, so everyone happily reached into the cake and took a candle.

I also took a candle, but when I licked the frosting from the bottom, my candle broke in half. I thought this was an omen that I might not make it to one hundred.

But who can be sure? Grandpa's death was never far from him. This is a story of how he could have died so many times, but somehow he just kept on living.

Introduction

Ever since I can remember, I've had the same nightmare. In the dream, I am running away, climbing out of windows, jumping over rooftops. I try to tell my parents that they need to hide, to run away, but no one listens to me. I am the only one who knows the future, but no one believes me. I argue, but I can't convince them.

When I wake up, my legs are stiff, my heart is pounding. Thank God that it was a dream, I think. Of course, it can't be real. It didn't happen to me.

My grandmother Tsilia, who died when I was a teenager, and my grandfather Shlomo were in a ghetto during the Second World War. Whenever they talked about it, they called it "a camp," but my father referred to it as "a ghetto." It was a place that had no gas chambers, but a place where the inhabitants were Jews, most of whom did not survive. What happened to them in the Ukrainian village of Obodovka, which was then under Romanian control, is a subject that they didn't talk about much. For many years, all I knew is that their parents, my great-grandparents, died there because they had nothing to eat.

When I consulted a reference book, I learned that between 9,000 and 10,000 Jews (most of them deported from Moldova, like my grandparents) were imprisoned at the Obodovka ghetto between the fall of 1941 and the spring of 1944. The ghetto was on land known as Transnistria—a portion of Ukraine that was controlled by Romania, which fought on Nazi Germany's side in the war.

Approximately 5,000 people died during the first year in the Obodovka ghetto, according to Alexander Kruglov's "The catastrophe of Ukrainian Jews 1941-1944." In the summer of 1942 and in the summer of 1943, about 1,860 people were sent from Obodovka to work in other towns, according to the reference book, which does not explain what happened to them.

By September of 1943, only 1,373 Jews were left at Obodovka—out of the 10,000 who had been sent there.

What happened to the Jews in the Obodovka ghetto? The Yad Vashem Central Database of Shoah Victims' Names, which is clearly incomplete, contains the names of only about one thousand Obodovka victims. The names come from testimonies submitted on behalf of the victims by their children, grandchildren, nieces, nephews and other relatives. The testimonies are handwritten in Yiddish, Hebrew, Russian and Romanian.

Sometimes a black and white photo is attached. I can only read the Russian testimonies, and I spent hours clicking through them, looking at the line that describes the cause of death. Most of the time, it says simply "hunger" or "hunger and cold" or "perished at the hands of Nazi tormentors" or "died as a result of unbearable living conditions in the ghetto." But a few testimonies are specific. Some say that the cause of death was typhoid, or that the victim died on the road on the way to the ghetto. One testimony said that the person was beaten to death by Romanian fascists. The testimony that stuck with me the most described the death of a child. It said that the child died from thirst. The person who submitted the testimony wrote that the child died from being left "without a drop of water."

Still, it should be pointed out that Jews had a better chance to survive under Romanian jurisdiction than in parts of Ukraine that were occupied by Germany. This was because Romania's fascist dictator, Ion Antonescu, ultimately refused to impose Hitler's Final Solution, despite the pressure from Nazi Germany. Romanian Jews were not sent by train to the gas chambers in Poland. Romanian soldiers in Transnistria did not have orders to execute every Jew. In fact, toward the end of the war, the conditions in the Obodovka ghetto improved. My grandmother said that most of those who survived the first terrible winter in the ghetto survived until the end of the war.

How did it happen that my grandparents were among the survivors when Obodovka was liberated by the Red Army in the spring of 1944?

My grandmother used to tell a story about a German soldier whom she knew in Obodovka. When my father retold the story that he heard from his mother, he said that the Jews were forbidden from leaving the camp under threat of being executed. Yet if they stayed, they would starve to death. But when my grandmother found a job in the village teaching a Ukrainian boy to read and write, a German soldier walked alongside her every day to make sure that she was safe on the road. The Ukrainian family gave my grandmother bread and sour cream, and this food saved her life.

My father remembers being surprised by this story, because when he was a teenager he didn't expect to hear that not all Germans were as heartless as they were portrayed in the Russian movies.

Everyone said that if I wanted to write about it, I should turn the story into a novel and invent the details.

But I am a journalist and I don't want to make anything up. It's easy enough to imagine a love story between a Jewish woman in the ghetto and a German soldier. But what I think makes my grandmother's story remarkable is that it isn't imaginary.

So I tried to learn more by searching in the archives and traveling to the places where my ancestors lived in Ukraine and Moldova. But mostly I ended up recording the stories I heard from my parents and grandparents, aunts and uncles. I wrote them down because I wanted to save other people's memories.

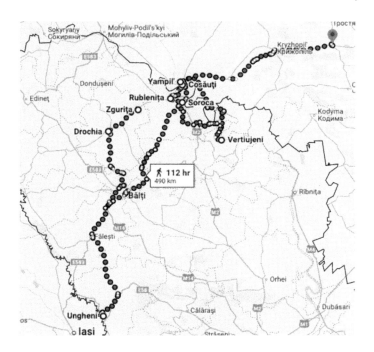

Above: A map of Moldova showing the death march of the Jews who were deported from Zguritsa (Zgurita) in July of 1941. The Jews of Zguritsa were forced to walk first to Drochia, then south to Ungheni on the Romanian border, then back north to Soroki (Soroca). From there, they walked to Iampil, Rublenita, the death camp at Vertiujeni, and the Cosauti forest, where approximately 150 men were shot. After that, they were forced into Ukraine, passing through Kryzhopil and finally arriving in Obodovka (Obodivka). This was a journey of approximately 500 kilometers on foot. (Google maps)

PART ONE

GRANDPA

How the War Started

"Do you remember how the war started, grandpa?" I asked my grandfather Shlomo, my father's father, when I came to visit him a few years ago. I had been working abroad and hadn't seen grandpa in about eight months.

Grandpa Shlomo was then living in a nursing home, where he claimed to be the oldest resident.

"Of course I remember," he said, as I took out my iPhone and focused it on his face, trying to keep my hand still so that the video wouldn't shake.

I wanted to make a recording of him talking about the Obodovka camp. Before, I never asked grandpa Shlomo about the war. Mostly, I didn't ask because I wasn't interested. And

I thought he'd be uncomfortable talking about it. But on that day, I felt that it was probably my last chance to talk to him.

By then, he was so old that his memories were all tangled up. He repeated himself a lot. It seemed that only the bare bones of his memories were left—all the details had been erased. He had to lean on his walker to shuffle between his bedroom and the nursing home's living room, where he spent hours sitting at a table with other seniors. He couldn't have conversations with them—because he didn't know English and the others in the nursing home couldn't speak Russian, Yiddish, Ukrainian or Romanian.

Grandpa Shlomo complained that he was bored because there was no one to talk with. But still he kept up his optimism. He said that he was thankful that his legs could hold him, his eyes could see, and his ears could hear. He said he was not like the other people in the nursing home, many of whom lay flat on their backs for much of the day.

Even though he had a bad memory, grandpa Shlomo never forgot what happened in the beginning of July of 1941, when Romanian Nazis came into Zguritsa, the Moldovan village where he lived.

In the morning, they came to take away the horses, grandpa said.

Then in the afternoon, all the Jews of Zguritsa were forced out of their homes at gunpoint.

"When we went outside, we were completely robbed," grandpa told us. "Even our clothes and our shoes were taken from us, and we were left only in our undergarments."

Together with the other Jews of Zguritsa, they were forced to walk for many days or weeks without food or shelter.

Grandpa Shlomo's father, Srul, walked ahead of everyone to beg for food. The people who pitied him gave him slices of bread.

As grandpa talked, I munched on a piece of crunchy chocolate waffle cake. Whenever anyone visited grandpa Shlomo, he made sure to have some sweets around. In his old apartment, there was always tea when guests came. In the nursing home, he couldn't boil water, so all he could offer us was water in plastic bottles.

The Rug that Hung on the Wall

Before grandpa Shlomo moved to the nursing home, he had a one-bedroom apartment in a building for elderly people not very far from the ocean. Grandpa had a small parrot in a birdcage above his dining room table, and on the wall he had hung a rug that he brought from Moldova. It depicted a deer grazing in a field. Grandpa also had a lot of family photographs of his children, grandchildren and great-grandchildren. He had a TV set that broadcast the Russian channel and he received a Russian newspaper.

At some point while living in his apartment, he started walking with a cane. But when he first got the cane, he was still strong. People joked that when they saw him walking down the street, he carried his cane under his arm, instead of using it to support himself like elderly people are supposed to. He used to walk to the synagogue every day.

But after some time, grandpa began having trouble with his blood pressure. When his blood pressure dropped suddenly, he would get dizzy and fall down. My father installed a video camera in the corner of grandpa's living room. Through the internet, it became possible for my father and a few other family members to observe what grandpa was up to at any time of the day or night. Not considering grandpa's privacy, my father thought himself very clever for this video-camera installation.

One day, my cousin Michael checked up on grandpa through the video camera and found him lying on the floor. It turned out that grandpa had fallen down the day before and could not get back up.

It was then that my father decided that grandpa should not stay in his apartment by himself anymore. He needed to be under supervision twenty-four hours a day.

Only a few of grandpa's things came with him to the nursing home. His room there had bare walls, and looked like a hospital room, intended only for temporary stays. He took with him only a few photographs, as well as his blanket and pillow. Grandpa Shlomo's and grandma Tsilia's china moved into our kitchen.

But what happened to the old rug with the deer that hung on grandpa's wall? My father says he wanted to bring the rug to grandpa's room in the nursing home—but the staff told him that rugs aren't permitted because of fire safety regulations.

Thrown Out of a Moving Train

When he first started telling us about his life, grandpa Shlomo began with his Romanian military service. He was drafted into the Romanian Army before World War Two—Zguritsa used to be part of Romania until 1940. What grandpa Shlomo remembered about the Romanian army is that if you brought your own horse then your military service was shorter. Grandpa came with his horse, and served in the Romanian army for two years, he said.

Grandpa had an older brother, Moishe, who was murdered while he served in the Romanian Army. He was thrown out of a moving train. Why did this happen? Grandpa Shlomo says it was an antisemitic attack. After the incident, great-grandfather Srul (grandpa Shlomo's father) went to the site of the murder, buried Moishe's body and built a monument to mark the spot.

I read that in the summer of 1940[1], after Romania succumbed to Soviet pressure and transferred Bessarabia (a region that was later incorporated into Moldova) to the Soviet Union, angry Romanian soldiers murdered Jews in retaliation. They also threw Jewish travelers, especially Jewish soldiers, from trains.

A year later, in the summer of 1941, when Nazi Germany invaded the Soviet Union, Romanian soldiers marched back into Moldova and took revenge on the Jews.

---

1   Moishe was killed near the town of Ungheni, which is on the border between Romania and Moldova.

The Zguritsa Pogrom

Romanian soldiers arrived in Zguritsa in the morning of July 3, 1941 with a crowd of non-Jews from the surrounding villages. It seemed that the Moldovans and the Ukrainians had been told in advance to come to Zguritsa to steal from the Jews. They walked into Jewish homes, taking everything that they wanted. They undressed the men and the women, saying, "I like your blouse, let me have it," or "I like your shoes, take them off." The Jews were left in their underclothes. They didn't undress the children, remembered Fira Oussatinski, a Jewish woman who survived.[1]

That morning, a group of Jews waited at the entrance to the village to welcome Romanian soldiers with bread and salt, according to custom. But when the soldiers arrived, someone yelled, "Don't eat Jewish bread!" and the horses knocked down the table that the Jews had set up. A Romanian officer then opened fire and the Jews ran for their lives, remembered Oleg Kandel, a survivor. [2]

Dozens or maybe hundreds of Jews were murdered that day. One man's head was cut off. A boy's stomach was cut open, Oussatinski said.[3] A Moldovan woman from Zguritsa remembered that the non-Jews showed the crosses that they wore around their necks to save themselves.

The next day, the Jews were forced out of their homes. They were told that they were going to be executed, but they were not killed. Instead, they were forced to stay outdoors without any food or water for days. They slept on the ground. Exhausted from the heat, they tried to sip water from the small puddles that were left in the ground from the horses' hooves. After dark, some Jewish children found a way into a cabbage field and ate all the cabbage.

Then the soldiers poured gasoline on the wooden homes and set the village ablaze.

Oussatinski remembered that Romanian soldiers started to rape Jewish women, but when the Germans arrived, they put an end to this.

My grandpa Shlomo did not say anything about women being raped and he did not see, or maybe did not remember, anyone being killed in Zguritsa on that day.

Or maybe he chose not to talk about it.

The Fruit Trees that Grew Along the Roads

Beaten with sticks, the expelled Jews of Zguritsa were forced to walk for many days without food.

"We were given nothing to eat, but the reason we did not starve is because fruit trees grow along the roads in Moldova," Oussatinski remembered. "We picked apples, pears, and plums. But we had no bread," she said.[4]

They slept outdoors, even as it rained, and on one occasion, the river overflowed.

Some people committed suicide.

Some mothers left their babies on the road, hoping someone would pick them up.

How My Grandfather Stole a Shoe

The weather was still warm in the summer when the Jews were forced out of Zguritsa, but their biggest problem was that they didn't have shoes, my grandfather said—because how far can you walk barefoot?

After about a week, they passed through a town called Soroca, on the banks of the Dniester River. It had been a town that had many Jewish residents, so during the war many houses were vacant. Grandpa Shlomo climbed into the cellar of one abandoned home, and there to his happiness he discovered a galosh. This shoe fitted him perfectly, he told us.

But when he went outside, grandpa Shlomo bumped into a man who was also wearing one shoe. He looked at the man's shoe and realized that the two shoes were from the same pair.

"Give me the galosh!" my grandfather said to the man, but the man refused.

Grandpa wanted to have two shoes instead of one, so when he noticed a Romanian policeman, he complained to him, "That man over there took my shoe and doesn't want to give it back!"

"Wait a minute, we'll sort this out," the policeman promised, and he walked over and asked the other man to show him the shoe.

When the policeman inspected the other man's shoe, he saw that the two shoes were from the same pair and he ordered the other man to give his shoe to my grandfather.

I thought this was the end of the story, but it turns out that grandpa got to wear those shoes only for a short time.

"We traded those shoes for fifteen kilograms of corn flour, because we had nothing to eat," he said. "We made polenta from the flour and it fed us for a month."

And that was one reason my grandfather did not die.

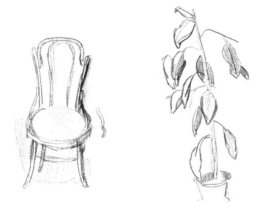

The Bird that Wanted to Be Free

When grandpa lived in his apartment in Lynn, Massachusetts, before he was sent into the nursing home, he owned a parakeet. The apartment was in a tall building for elderly people, and grandpa had a one bedroom with a living room and a small kitchen. You had to walk through the bedroom to get to the bathroom, which had a sliding door that did not lock, which was why I didn't like using it. In the small living room stood a couch, a dining table, and a television set. The parakeet lived in a cage near the window.

Sometimes grandpa would let the bird out, and it would perch on the top of the bedroom door, unwilling to return to its small prison. Grandpa didn't know what to do about it, so he would call my father for help.

"The parrot doesn't want to go back in the cage!" he'd say on the phone.

"So put some food in there to lure him," my father advised.

"I did already!" grandpa would reply.

"When did you put the food in the cage?"

"Three days ago!"

Grandpa's bird preferred to go hungry for days, rather than stay in prison. (Or maybe he found other sources of food, or snuck into the cage when grandpa was asleep? Or maybe the story about the parakeet was just grandpa's strategy to get my father to visit?)

In any case, whenever the parrot revolted against its unhappy fate, my father would drive to grandpa's apartment during his lunch break, catch the poor bird, and put it back behind metal bars.

When grandpa moved to the nursing home, the parrot moved in with his next-door neighbor, a lady I don't remember meeting, but someone who came to grandpa's funeral years later.

"Why didn't you take the parakeet?" I asked my father when he told the story.

"You know," he started to say, coming up with an excuse. "It's a lot of work to take care of a bird."

How the Youngest Brother Died

Grandpa Shlomo was sleeping when I came to see him at the nursing home a few weeks later. Maybe he wasn't asleep but he was lying down on his bed with all his clothes but without his shoes, and I didn't know if his eyes were open or closed. It was about seven o'clock in the evening and it wasn't yet dark. I left the room, not wishing to disturb him. I hesitated about what to do, so I called my father and he said, "Go inside and wake him up, it's too early for him to be sleeping."

When I came in, grandpa took my hand and tried to sit up in bed—and I could see that he was glad that I came. He started telling me stories. It didn't help to ask questions, it was better to just listen to the memories that came into his mind.

That's how I found out that grandpa Shlomo had a brother about whom I never heard before. Grandpa Shlomo's youngest brother was named Aizic. When Aizic was born, he had a twin, but the twin, whose name grandpa can't remember now, died when he was a toddler. Aizic also died young. According to grandpa, Aizic's life ended while they were all forced to walk from Zguritsa to Obodovka, Ukraine, a distance of more than one hundred kilometers.

One day, a Romanian policeman announced that he needed a group of 150 people for a work assignment. Those Jews (and grandpa Shlomo's youngest brother Aizic was with them) were taken away and never seen again, grandpa told me. Aizic was only 19 years old.

At the end of the war, grandpa Shlomo returned to the place where he last saw his brother and asked the villagers about what happened. They told him that they saw that the Jews were forced to dig a pit, and when they finished digging, they were lined up around the pit and the Romanian policeman—"an evil, heartless man," grandpa added as he told the story—fired at them with his machine gun. Some were killed and some fell into the pit even though they were only injured. They were buried anyway, and the soil in the pit shifted up and down for three days until all became still.

"That's how we knew that we didn't need to look for Aizic after the war ended," grandpa said.

Grandpa Shlomo also said that when they took away his little brother Aizic, the Nazis could have taken him too, but he ducked down and hid behind something, so they didn't notice him.

And that was the second reason he didn't die.

The Airport and the Hospital

A few years ago, before grandpa Shlomo came to live at the nursing home, he was really sick. One day, he gave me a photograph of himself with a one hundred dollar bill inside a white envelope. On the envelope, he tried to write a note, a goodbye note. He started in Russian, but switched to Yiddish, which I don't speak and can't read. He spent a long time writing, bent over the table, but when we asked him to read aloud what he had written, he could not. He repeated himself, as if, having written a word, he had forgotten that he had.

"From your grandfather, from your grandfather, from your grandfather," he wrote three times in a row.

"I should have written this note a year ago," he said to my mother with regret.

That day, we sat down at the table and had nothing to say to each other. As always, when he was better, grandfather offered us tea and candy. We pretended to eat even if we had just finished our breakfast at home and were neither hungry nor thirsty. The filling inside the chocolate candy stuck to my teeth. Grandpa was sipping his tea from a teaspoon, bringing it to his lips. He had trouble swallowing. He couldn't name the year or the month. He had forgotten how old he was.

"A couple of months more or a couple of months less," he said. "It makes no difference."

That day, my father asked grandpa Shlomo how much sugar he wanted in his tea. Grandpa always liked three teaspoons of sugar in his cup, which is a lot of sugar, but it never did him any harm.

"Yes, old age is hard," he said as he looked at my 55-year-old mother.

"Does anything hurt, grandpa?" I asked.

"Not really," he said. "But if it's not one thing, it's something else. My heart hurts. My legs won't hold me anymore. And then the boredom, the boredom."

My mother looked at him, and I wondered, if she thought about her own impending old age, the old age that neither she, nor anyone else can escape. And I felt tears come to my eyes, but it was not because of my grandfather's suffering, but because I imagined what would happen to my mother thirty years in the future.

"Why don't you try reading a book, grandpa?" I suggested. "You know they have books with big letters. Where is your Bible?"

I noticed that day that the newspaper lay unopened on his kitchen table. He probably cannot read it anymore, I thought. Maybe he can't follow the story, because his mind is so clouded. He outlived most of his friends. Even his doctor passed away. I guess he just sits in his chair all day, looking at the wall with the photos, remembering the past. He has a lot to remember.

The following weekend, my father brought grandpa Shlomo to the emergency room again. That time, grandpa fell down in the middle of the night and broke his wrist. They waited in the hospital for eight hours until a doctor saw them.

"How long will we be waiting in this airport?" grandfather asked.

"We are not in the airport," my father replied. "We are at the hospital."

Grandpa Shlomo said he understood, but five minutes later he asked about the airport again.

Then grandfather said, without warning, "We have to sell all the wine before it goes bad."

"Yes we should do that," my father replied, even though there was no wine. "I already found a buyer."

"Who is it?" grandfather asked, curious. Then he said, "You must keep the house warm at night. That's the most important thing. Keep the house warm."

"Yes I will," my father replied.

It was the end of June.

The Selection

After weeks and weeks of walking, the Jews of Zguritsa came to a place where the soldiers sat at a table and they told some people to go to the left and others to go to the right. Those who went in the direction of Mogilev Podolskiy were all murdered. Those who were sent to Transnistria, where my grandparents went, were not murdered right away but forced into a camp.

"We will not kill you, but we will make your life so bad that you'll wish that you were dead," one survivor remembered hearing a soldier say to her.[5]

When the selection took place, no one knew that the difference between left and right was the difference between life and death.

Just by chance, my grandfather was sent in the direction of life, and that was the third reason he did not die.

Villages at Dusk

Every time we visit him, grandpa Shlomo offers us food. Today he gave us bananas and an apple, and showed us the cake that he is saving in the fridge for my brother and my brother's new wife.

"Thank you for coming to see me!" he repeated several times. "I am very bored here. I wish I had tried to learn at least a little English after I came to America. I really like talking to people."

Lately, he took up painting, or coloring, which is an activity that is offered in the nursing home.

All of grandpa Shlomo's pictures look like villages at dusk. The houses are dark blue, the streets look like the sun has just set, and there isn't any light in any of the windows. Maybe he paints villages from the time before electricity existed.

The Frozen Bodies

At the Obodovka camp in Ukraine, where my grandfather ended up with his family after walking hundreds of kilometers barefoot, the Jews suffered much from hunger and from the cold. The place had been an animal farm before the war. The Jews had no winter clothes and they were housed in cowsheds and pigsties with caved-in roofs and without glass in the windows. They slept on the ground. If someone got a little food, he or she ate it so that no one saw them. They had no place to bathe. They had lice. The lice spread typhus.

During the first winter, more than half of the people in the camp died. Rats ate the faces of the corpses. Even so, those who were alive were jealous of those who were already dead.

Some said that every day as many as forty people died. Survivors remembered that there was a heap of frozen corpses in the corner of the dark cowshed. Some said it was so because the Romanians did not allow the Jews to bury the dead.[6] There was a Jewish cemetery in Obodovka, but it was about three kilometers away from the camp, and the Romanians did not allow the Jews to go there.

Others said the bodies were not buried because the ground was frozen and burial was impossible. Grandpa Shlomo said that in the winter when the ground was frozen, the people in the camp were too weak to bury the dead. They piled the corpses into one corner of the cowshed and only when there were ten bodies, they would carry them away.

When the starving men finally took away the frozen bodies, they laid them down outside and snow fell on them. In the spring, when the snow melted, dogs carried away their bones.

The corpses were naked, because those who carried them away took their clothes. Clothes and shoes could be exchanged for food in the village. Some survivors said that the corpse collectors were the only ones who always had enough to eat.

The Nazi Who Rode a Motorcycle

One of the scariest stories I heard about Obodovka is about a German policeman who used to tie people to the back of his motorcycle and drag them behind until they were dead.

"Because the streets in Obodovka were not asphalted, but cobblestone, after half a kilometer, nothing remained of the victim," said Petr Roitman, an Obodovka survivor who was interviewed in 1995.[7]

One day, I heard a similar story from my father's friend Borik, whose parents survived the Holocaust in Bershad, a town that is 26 kilometers from Obodovka.

"Every day, he would choose a boy around fourteen or fifteen years old and tie him to the back of his motorcycle. While he still could, the boy would run behind the motorcycle. Then he would fall, and he would be dragged behind until nothing was left of him," Borik said.

My father could not listen to this.

"Please stop," he said to Borik. "You will give us bad dreams."

Why Did Haim Come Back?

My grandfather recently told us that he had an older brother named Haim.

Before the war, Haim and grandpa Shlomo worked together as grain merchants. They used to buy wheat, sunflower seeds and corn from farmers and resell everything at the railroad station in another town, about 20 kilometers away.

Haim was strong, so when the Jews were forced to move into a ghetto after weeks of marching through towns and villages, he got some Romanian clothes from somewhere and ran away. (The Jews and the Romanians dressed differently in those days, grandpa explained.) My grandfather asked him where he was going to go, and Haim told him he was going back to Zguritsa because he had non-Jewish friends there, people he used to do business with. The ghetto did not have a fence around it, so one day Haim left.

After Haim disappeared, policemen came to question grandpa Shlomo.

"Where is your older brother?" they yelled.

But all grandpa Shlomo said to them was that Haim went away, but where he went he didn't know.

About six months later, at the end of winter, Haim returned to the Obodovka camp. When he came back, he was so thin that grandpa Shlomo barely recognized him.

"Where have you been?" he asked Haim.

Haim told him that he wanted to walk back to Zguritsa, and to do that he planned to cross over the Dniester River when it froze over in the winter. But along the way he became weak and couldn't go any further.

He met an old Ukrainian man who agreed to hide him in his house. At that time, hiding a Jew was very risky. If the Nazis found out, they could take revenge on the whole family, murdering everyone. At first Haim stayed at the Ukrainian man's house and worked for him. But when Haim became ill, the old man told him to leave. He didn't want Haim to die inside his house, grandpa Shlomo said.

"Go back home," the Ukrainian man told Haim—so Haim walked back to the Obodovka camp.

After Haim returned to the ghetto, he lay down and would not get up. It was very cold in the cowshed, and Haim didn't even have a blanket. He lost the will to live, my grandfather said. A few weeks later, he died.

When I heard this story, I couldn't stop thinking about why Haim returned to a place where people were being starved to death.

The Unlucky Wedding

The only other known detail about Haim—except for the way he died—is that he had an unlucky wedding.

That's because Haim's grandmother, Gitl Koyfman (who was also my grandfather's grandmother, of course), unexpectedly passed away on Haim's wedding day. She wasn't ill, grandpa Shlomo says, but one day she suddenly died. This day happened to be Haim's wedding day. To keep the unfortunate event from ruining a happy occasion, someone in the family decided not to announce grandmother's death until the wedding was over. Grandma was dead, but everyone just kept dancing and celebrating.

"But if Haim was married then what happened to his wife in Obodovka?" I asked when I heard this story.

Grandmother's death on Haim's wedding day was a bad omen, grandpa Shlomo replied—and indeed his married life was not a happy one. Haim and his wife separated not long after they got married.

Grandpa Shlomo never asked Haim why his wife left him. It was a private matter and he didn't pry, he said.

During the war, Haim's wife and her two brothers ended up in another town and no one heard anything from them after the war. In all likelihood all of them died, grandpa Shlomo said.

Barefoot in the Snow

Grandpa Shlomo's older brother Haim and his father Srul (my great grandfather) died at around the same time. I think it was probably in the beginning of 1942 at the end of winter.

But the first one to die in the ghetto was grandpa Shlomo's uncle. He died from some kind of stomach illness.

"Was it typhoid?" I wanted to know.

But grandpa Shlomo didn't know the word "typhoid" in Russian, so he couldn't reply to my question. Perhaps it was not typhoid, but dysentery.

"A stomach illness," he said. "They told my uncle he should eat yogurt. His wife tried to get yogurt for him. But nothing helped him."

This uncle, grandpa Shlomo's mother's brother, was named Yosef Koyfman and he was an extraordinary man, grandpa Shlomo said. Before the war, he traveled to Argentina. But unfortunately, he decided to return to Moldova and ended up dying in the Holocaust when he was only 50 years old.

"And how did your father die, grandpa?" I asked.

"I will tell you," grandpa Shlomo said, which is the way he often began his stories.

But actually grandpa Shlomo has two versions of his father's death—and maybe there is truth in both.

In one version of the story, grandpa Shlomo claims that his father died from a broken heart. It just so happened that grandpa Shlomo's mother, named Haya-Sara (in the Romanian records her name is listed as Sura), fell ill just before the start of the war. Grandpa Shlomo's older brother Yasha brought her to the hospital in the town of Chernivtsi, in Ukraine. She died in that hospital because there was no medicine, grandpa Shlomo says. But grandpa Shlomo's father didn't get the news of his wife's death until later. By the time he found out that his wife passed away, he was in the ghetto.

"He said, 'I can't go on living without her,' and not long after that he died," grandpa Shlomo told me.

But according to another version of grandpa Shlomo's memory, one winter day his father Srul went to the ghetto canteen, even though he didn't have any shoes. It then started snowing and he had to walk back barefoot in the snow.

"He caught a cold and died," grandpa Shlomo said.

Grandpa Wants to Go Outside

The nursing home staff don't allow grandpa to go outside by himself anymore. They say that one time he went out and got lost. The nursing home has a secret code for the elevator so that patients can't ride it. So now grandpa has to wait until someone has a chance to take him outside.

"You can't go for a walk now, there is too much snow," my father told grandpa the last time we visited, probably to make him feel that he wasn't missing out on anything. "No one is walking in this weather. Plus if you go out in the freezing cold, you could catch pneumonia."

The entire winter, grandpa has only been outside once, my father said. My father only found the time once this winter to leave work early and take him outside before sunset.

Grandpa just wants to go outside and sit on a bench, breathe the fresh air, and watch the world. He also wants to go to a store, my father said. He hasn't been to a store in years. They don't take people shopping when they live in the nursing home.

"What does he need to buy?" I asked my father, when he told the story.

"He doesn't need to buy anything," my father said. "He just wants to go to a store and look around."

Two Buckets of Potatoes and a Broken Bottle

Before he died, my great-grandfather Srul showed grandpa Shlomo a trail that he found in the forest. This trail led from the Obodovka camp into the village. Grandpa Shlomo says he would get up two hours before dawn and walk to the village where an elderly Ukrainian couple waited for him with breakfast. They ate mostly eggs and potatoes, because they kept chickens and grew potatoes. In exchange, grandpa Shlomo carried water from the well for them, and chopped firewood.

"They were good people," grandpa Shlomo said. "They never sat down to eat breakfast without me."

With the money he earned, grandpa would go to the village market and buy two buckets of potatoes. He would put the potatoes into a bag, tie this bag around his shoulders like a backpack, and walk back to the cowshed where the Jews were held.

When he returned to the camp each day, everyone was already looking out of the window and waiting for him.

"What do you have today, Shlomo?" they asked.

"Potatoes and a little corn flour," he'd reply.

Grandpa says that he would bring enough food for everyone—three or four potatoes per person. (Although I am not sure who he means when he says "everyone.") He also said that he sold the potatoes for a little money, but I don't understand how the Jews in the camp had any money. I do know that they managed to build a stove in the cowshed. They warmed up next to this stove at night, grandpa Shlomo's sister Polina baked the potatoes, and they ate them without salt.

One time, my grandfather was stopped in the center of the village by Romanian policemen. It was easy to tell him apart from the others, grandpa Shlomo said, because of the way he was dressed. He had nothing but a long black coat on, tied at the waist with a rope.

"What are you doing here, Jew?" the policemen yelled at him. "If we see you again, we'll kill you!"

And then a policeman hit my grandpa on the head with a bottle. The glass bottle broke against my grandfather's head, but he was not hurt, he said, "because Romanian glass was very thin and of poor quality."

After that, grandpa Shlomo still went to the village every day, but he stayed away from the center where he saw the police.

He never ran into those policemen again, and this was another reason he did not die.

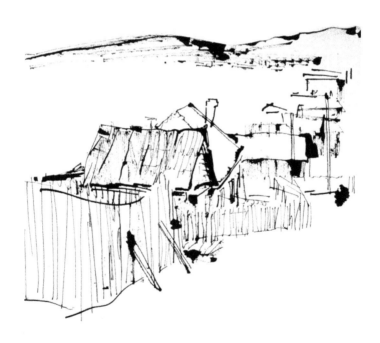

If They Didn't Have Bread, They Gave Potatoes

The next time I visited, I asked grandpa, "How are you going to celebrate your one hundredth birthday?"

It was Passover Seder. Grandpa was sitting at the table between his son and his daughter and he was looking good in his holiday suit and his striped red tie. He looked better now than a year ago, I thought. On his head, he wore a red baseball cap.

Grandpa Shlomo didn't reply to my question directly, but this is what he said:

"I will be one hundred years old soon! People ask me why I'm still alive. Most people are dead before they get to my age," he began. "The reason I am alive is because I did a lot of good things when I was young."

"He says that God is keeping him here," my mother chimed in.

"In the camp, there were a lot of people who were sick," grandpa said. "I used to go out two hours before sunrise, and I would go knocking on doors in the village. People gave me their stale bread. In the ghetto, people soaked this bread in water and that's what they ate."

"Did all the Ukrainians give you food? Or was it one family in particular that helped you?" I asked grandpa.

He didn't answer my question, but just continued saying what he wanted to say.

"I learned how to speak Ukrainian," he said. "I just walked along the edge of the village, away from where the police was. I knocked on doors and asked for bread."

"Did some people refuse to give?" I asked.

"If they didn't give bread, they gave potatoes," grandpa said.

"Did they know that the food was for the Jews?"

"Of course they knew," grandpa said.

Adam and Eve

One day, when I visited grandpa Shlomo, he started to tell me the story about Adam and Eve.

"Oh no! This is going to be a waste of time," I thought when he began summarizing the first chapter of the Bible.

But grandpa Shlomo had his own version of Adam and Eve.

"Eve wanted to go for a walk in the town to look around, but how could she go there when she had no clothes and she was completely naked?" grandpa Shlomo said. "So she took the leaves from the trees and she attached the leaves together to make some clothes for herself!"

Grandpa's story made me think of the Jews in the Obodovka ghetto: They needed to go into the village to look for some food, but they had no clothes. Their clothes and their shoes had been stolen from them, and in the wintertime it was very cold.

But unlike Adam and Eve, they didn't live in the Garden of Eden.

How Grandpa Saved His Brother

At some point between 1941 and 1944, grandpa Shlomo saved his older brother's life.

When the war started, grandpa Shlomo's brother Yasha was in the town of Chernivtsi because he brought his mother to the hospital there. There was a big Jewish hospital in Chernivtsi. That's why he ended up in a different location from the rest of the family. Somehow, during the war, grandpa Shlomo got word of Yasha's whereabouts.

Grandpa Shlomo hired a Ukrainian man to dress his brother up in peasant clothes and drive him to Obodovka from the other town in a horse-pulled sleigh. He said he gave the Ukrainian one hundred dollars for this. Maybe he meant one hundred rubles or one hundred lei or whatever currency was in use at that time.

"Had Yasha remained in the other place, he would not have survived," grandpa Shlomo said.

When I heard this story about how grandpa Shlomo saved his brother Yasha, I thought if they could dress in Ukrainian clothes and arrange for transportation, if the camp didn't have a fence around it, why didn't all of them escape?

I tried to ask grandpa about this, but it seemed that his memories were made up of stories that he had retold many times, and he couldn't find the answers to the questions that he hadn't already answered before.

"We stayed in Obodovka," is all that he said.

Forced Labor

The Jews in Obodovka were forced to go on work assignments.

A survivor named Petr Roitman recounted how he worked in the beet and potato fields.

"The overseers were behind us. If someone stopped working for a second, he would be hit with a whip," he testified[8].

Another time, the Germans wanted an outdoor area for dancing, so they made the Jews stomp around on the ground barefoot for four hours to flatten out the soil.

On another occasion, the Jews were forced to work on the construction of a Ukrainian church. They had to carry bricks to the top. One day, a man fell from the church steeple and dislocated his leg[9].

Most importantly, the Jews in the Obodovka camp had to avoid being sent to labor assignments to the parts of Ukraine which were under German control and meant certain death.

One time, it was announced that four hundred men from Obodovka would be sent to Nikolayev, where the Germans were building a bridge. Those who went there did not return.

My grandpa Shlomo avoided being sent there, and this is another reason he did not die.

How Curiosity Saved Grandpa

One time, my father asked grandpa what gave him the strength to keep going in the ghetto. My father must have asked this question around the time when he was reading a book by a concentration camp survivor who talked about how the death rate in the camps skyrocketed after important holidays. It was, the author of the book explained, because people would force themselves to live as long as they had something to look forward to, like a holiday. But once a benchmark was behind them, they often lost the will to keep going. The desire to live was of foremost importance, the author concluded.

So when my father was reading this book, he asked grandpa what gave him strength during the war.

Grandpa Shlomo replied that he wanted to live to find out who would win the war.

It was curiosity that kept him going.

The Collective Farm

My grandfather says he was lucky because one day someone in Obodovka asked, "Who wants to work?" and he volunteered.

On the collective farm called Dubino, which was about three kilometers from the Obodovka camp, the Jews who were strong enough to work were fed two times per day with borscht and bread. The work involved taking care of animals, slaughtering pigs, and digging wells. The Jews who worked at this farm did not starve. That's why my father says that the man who ran this farm was probably someone like Oskar Schindler.

But later, according to one version of the past in grandpa's memory, they had to leave the farm because another group of

Jews had given bribes to take their spots. Grandpa said he was such a good worker, that the director of the farm begged him to stay. The director warned him, "Don't leave, they will kill you!" But grandpa replied that he would only stay if his whole family was permitted to remain with him.

"If they die, I will die with them," he said.

When he told this story, grandpa said that if he hadn't volunteered to work on the farm, he would not have survived that first winter in Obodovka.

Not Like Schindler

Was the director of the Dubino farm, whose last name was Zaslotskii, a man who can be compared to Oskar Schindler? Other survivors did not remember him in such a way.

One survivor said the first thing she saw when she arrived at Dubino were two men suspended by their feet from the gates. They were alive, and they were hanging upside-down. A small fire was burning beneath them—with a flame that was not large enough to allow the men to die quickly[10].

But another survivor who also worked on the farm said that when they arrived, they were greeted with a warm meal on tables that were covered by tablecloths, and everyone was very happy and grateful[11]. They were housed in a long building and every family was given a bed. But for some reason, the next day, the beds were taken away and the Jews were given hay instead. Like animals, they had to sleep in the hay, with rats and mice running on the floor. A former inmate remembered that on the Dubino farm, the Jews were forced to harvest corn in the winter. They walked barefoot in the snow, picking corn from the snow with their bare hands. [12]

But later the conditions on the Dubino farm allegedly improved. At one point, survivors remembered, a man by the name of Chuhaz began to leave the doors of the storage room open, which the Jews took as a hint to help themselves to potatoes, beets, animal feed, and sunflower seeds.

"Do whatever you need to do, I will pretend that I didn't see anything," said this man.

So the Jews took the food and ate it. Later, a canteen was set up on the farm, and people were given bread and soup.

How I Wore Grandpa's Sweatpants

The last time when I visited grandpa Shlomo in the nursing home, he was in the common room watching television with the other seniors—except he was the only one who was awake.

When he saw me, grandpa was overjoyed.

"You came!" he exclaimed. "You promised you would come today and here you are!"

As usual, I asked him many questions about the war, but halfway during the conversation he switched the subject and said, "You know, I have to tell you, I have been thinking about you since this morning!"

"Really?" I asked.

"Yes," he said. "Now you are at the age when you should think seriously about getting married. I want to tell your parents about this also. If you can't meet someone by yourself, you should put an ad into the newspaper. No need to write that you are thirty-two years old. Just say that you are thirty."

I didn't tell him that I was already 34. I didn't say that I am already registered on several dating sites.

Then grandpa asked me to get the chocolate waffle cake and break a piece off for myself. Knives are not allowed in the nursing home. So we broke chunks of cake off with our hands, and pieces of chocolate fell on the carpet.

When the air-conditioner made the room too cold, grandpa fumbled around in his chest of drawers and found a pair of sweatpants.

"Put these on," he told me. "They are clean."

I was not cold, but arguing with grandpa was useless.

"Put them on, or you'll catch a cold," he said.

I pulled on the pair of pants on top of my shorts, and when it was time to leave, it was very hard to convince grandpa to take his pants back. He wanted me to have them as a gift.

"Don't worry, grandpa, I have heat in the car," I finally said. "And next time when I come to see you, I can put these pants on again in case I get cold."

The Partisans Who Dressed as Nazis

In 1943, the Dubino farm was raided by a group of partisans. The partisans took away the best horses, cows and pigs and some Jewish men, and they left some salt and flour for the Jewish workers.

"Try to survive, we'll come back and rescue you," the partisans said to the Jews.

The message the partisans left to the Romanians and the Germans was that "if you touch the Jews, we will burn your farm down."

Some survivors remembered that the partisans raided Dubino many times, so much that the Germans and the Romanians were afraid to go there.

Partisans also visited the Obodovka ghetto.

A survivor named Petr Roitman, who was a child in the ghetto, was very surprised one day when he saw about forty or fifty cars with German machine guns drive into town. A soldier dressed in an SS uniform called him over in German and, as he approached the car fearing for his life, the soldier gave him a loaf of bread and some meat.

"What a strange German soldier," the Jewish boy thought.

Later he found out that the man who gave him bread and spoke to him in German was not from the SS, but one of the partisans who dressed up in Nazi uniform as a disguise.

The Soldiers With Feathers

Other than the German and the Romanian soldiers, survivors from the Obodovka camp and the Dubino farm also remembered the Italians.

Italian soldiers wore feathers on their helmets. The Italians didn't see much difference between a Ukrainian and a Jew. They treated everyone the same, survivors said.

One time, three German soldiers in the Obodovka camp were dragging away a Jewish girl to rape her. Just then, lucky for her, a group of Italian soldiers was passing by. When the Italians saw what was happening, they fought the Germans and freed the girl, according to a survivor who witnessed the incident[13].

On another occasion, in the nearby town of Chechelnik, the Italians slaughtered a cow, but shared some of the meat with the Jewish children, a survivor remembered[14]. Italians also gave the Jews bread and chocolate.

In another strange incident involving Italians, some survivors remembered that a few Italian deserters came to the Dubino farm toward the end of the war and asked the Jews to hide them because they did not want to fight in the war anymore. The Romanian language which the Moldovan Jews spoke is similar to Italian, so they must have understood each other. Those Italians took some Jewish women back to Italy with them as wives, a survivor said[15].

Never Too Old to Dance

My parents say that the nursing home where grandpa lives looks more like a hotel than a hospital.

Maybe they just say that to make themselves feel good.

In Russia, sending someone to a nursing home was considered a cruel thing to do. It was something children were never supposed to do to their parents. I don't know of any of our other relatives, great-grandparents or great-great-parents, who lived or died in nursing homes. But this is America, everyone is busy here. No one has the time to care for their elderly parents. Besides, my parents say, the nursing home saved grandpa Shlomo's life. Had he stayed at home, they say, he would have been dead by now. Who could take care of him as well as the trained nurses over there—making sure that he takes all his medicines at the right hours, that his blood pressure never gets too high or too low, that all his liquids have thickeners added to them so that he doesn't choke? My parents have jobs. They can't supervise grandpa all day long.

Still, grandpa's only wish is to live at home with his daughter or with his son. He doesn't stop asking my father and my aunt to take him home. He says he wants to work in our garden, to take care of our tomato plants. But my father only brings grandpa to visit on holidays. On these rare occasions, grandpa dresses up in his suit and tie and almost no one can guess, from looking at him, that he is almost one hundred years old.

Grandpa likes to dance. Whenever he hears music, he gets up to join everyone on the dance floor. Sometimes people are surprised when they see an old man like grandpa dancing.

His biggest wish is to dance at my wedding, but my wish is to see him dance at his own one hundredth birthday party.

How Grandpa Milled Grain

One day, when grandpa Shlomo was walking from the Obodovka camp to the village, he found a piece of metal. It was a circular piece from the middle of a wheel—not the wheel of a car but the wheel that was used for horse-pulled carriages. He picked up the metal part and brought it with him.

On another occasion, he came across another piece of metal. This time the piece was elongated, and it came from a plow or a rake.

The piece had to be exactly the right size, and this one was. When he put the straight part into the circular part, he found that he could use this contraption to mill grain into flour, my father said.

During the war, milling grain into flour was a service that was needed in Obodovka. Maybe the flour mill that had been used before the war was no longer functional, maybe it had been destroyed or could not be used without electricity. In any case, my father says, grandpa Shlomo built a hand-operated device to mill grain.

Later during the course of the war, when conditions for the Jews in the Obodovka ghetto improved, grandpa, his brother Yasha, and sister Polia would buy some grain in the market, mill it into flour by hand and resell it—keeping a little for their own consumption.

And that was how they survived.

Have a Good Year

One time, when we came to visit grandpa Shlomo, my father spoke to him in Yiddish.

I never heard my father speak Yiddish before. Mostly he understands Yiddish, but he can't speak it that well.

When my father was a little boy, grandpa Shlomo and grandma Tsilia would speak Yiddish among themselves if they didn't want my father to know what they were talking about.

Nowadays grandpa doesn't have anyone to speak Yiddish with.

When we were leaving, grandpa walked us to the elevator, pushing his walker ahead of himself. It made a loud noise, scraping against the carpeted floor. As the elevator doors were about to close, my father said, "Good night!" to grandpa in

Yiddish. I understood "good night," because Yiddish sounds like German, and German sounds like English.

I also heard that grandpa didn't say "good night" back. His reply sounded like something different.

"What did he say?" I asked my father after the elevator doors closed. "You said, 'Good night,' and he said, 'Good luck'?"

"No," my father said. "He said, 'Have a good year!'"

My father explained that this is the traditional Yiddish answer when someone wishes you a good night.

I guess when a language disappears, a unique way of thinking vanishes with it.

PART TWO

GRANDMA

From Romania to The Soviet Union

In the summer or early fall of 1940, my grandma Tsilia's family crossed the border from Romania into the Soviet Union. At that time, my grandmother was around 23 years old. Like other Romanian Jews, her family was fleeing antisemitism, running from attacks like the one in which my grandfather's brother Moishe was murdered.

But a trip to the cinema also influenced their decision to leave Romania. Grandma Tsilia told my father that her family was inspired to come to the USSR after watching a Russian movie. It was probably a Soviet propaganda film about how wonderful life was in the USSR, where all ethnic groups had equal rights and there were no rich or poor people.

Before 1940, grandma Tsilia's family lived in Iasi, one of the largest cities in Romania. It was a modern town with electric lights. The city had many synagogues. Grandma Tsilia worked in a bookstore. Her father Abram Gelman owned a shop that sold household goods and rugs. He was not very successful in business - every time he bought something, hoping to resell it for a higher price, prices would fall and he would lose his money, I heard family members say. Still, he was well respected in the community, so much so that people went to him for advice. Grandma Tsilia was very beautiful, and several wealthy men asked for her hand in marriage. But her father refused them all, saying that he would not marry his daughter off to a merchant.

But as everyone often imagines, the grass is greener on the other side—so one day grandma Tsilia's family sold their house and all their possessions and walked across the border into the Soviet Union.

It's an interesting historical detail, I think, because we often hear stories about Jews trying to get out of the Soviet Union, but not about Jews illegally crossing the border to get into the communist country.

But after arriving in the USSR, they discovered that life wasn't like the movie. Grandma Tsilia used to say that her father regretted leaving Romania, but at the start of the war, in July of 1941, a third of Iasi's Jewish population (13,266 people) were massacred. Many others were deported to concentration camps. Had she stayed in Iasi, my grandmother might not have survived the war.

The Ticket to America

Even before grandma Tsilia walked from Romania to the Soviet Union, her life could have turned out differently.

That's because a year after the Titanic sank, her family could have come to the United States. In 1913, grandma Tsilia's father Abram Gelman had a US visa and a boat ticket in hand. It was a ticket to Chicago, where his brothers were already settled.

But before he could board the steamer, Abram was introduced to his future wife, Perl. Perl refused the transatlantic journey. The reason, my father's cousin explained, was that Abram was very good-looking and a very good singer, while Perl considered her own appearance only average. She feared that her husband would run off with another woman in

America. So they stayed in Europe and 28 years later would both die from starvation in the Obodovka ghetto.

The Uncle Who Sold Bagels

One day, when we were talking about how little we know about grandma Tsilia's side of the family, my father remembered a story about uncle Shaya, who was as plump as a pig.

"Uncle Shaya must have been a butcher. That's why he was so fat," my father said.

"He wasn't a butcher," aunt Polina interrupted. "You know why he was fat? He owned a bakery in Soroca."

On April 9, 1932, there was a big flood in Soroca, as the snow melted and the Dniester River overflowed its banks. Many people lost their homes. The whole city was in panic. Even the *New York Times* reported on the disaster, writing that "total destruction of the town was feared."

That day, uncle Shaya stood on the flooded street in his rubber boots, selling his freshly baked bagels.

"All the stores were closed. People didn't know where to get food. And he was out there, calling out—'Bagels! Warm bagels!'" aunt Polina said, repeating a story she must have heard from grandma Tsilia. "He saw it as a business opportunity."

When my father talked about uncle Shaya, he described him so vividly that I assumed he must have met him in person. But my father never met this uncle.

Uncle Shaya, along with his wife[2], who was my great-grandmother's sister, and their daughter were all murdered in the Holocaust.

---

2   Her name was Inda Stepankovskaya and the daughter's name was Doba.

Ten Years for Telling a Joke

Grandma Tsilia had two brothers and a sister. When the war started, all of her siblings evacuated ahead of the advancing Nazi armies. Grandma's brother, Misha, went to Kuibyshev. Sister Sabina made it to Stalingrad. And brother Sava, also known in the family as Sauliko, went to Tomsk, in Siberia. My grandmother Tsilia was the one who stayed behind with her parents because she was the oldest in the family.

Grandma's family was renowned for telling jokes and funny stories, and this talent passed down to my father, too. But back then, during the Stalin era, all this joking was dangerous. So allow me to say a few words about my great-uncle Sava, and how he got in trouble for telling a joke.

Sometime during the war, Sava was drafted into the Red Army, and as he was riding in the train from Siberia to the front lines, he started entertaining the other passengers with his funny anecdotes. It was a very long journey, and everyone gets bored on long train journeys. Unfortunately, one of the jokes he told must have had an anti-Soviet flavor to it, and someone reported it to the authorities. Sava was arrested at one of the stations and removed from the train. A military tribunal sentenced him to ten years—for telling a joke! He was sent to a gulag in Magadan, which is in the Far East.

And that's how uncle Sava avoided fighting in the war, and ended up getting married to a woman he met in a prisoner camp in the Far East. In the mid-1950s, after Stalin died, Sava returned to Moldova with his wife, Gilda—bringing along a recipe for Siberian dumplings.

I have a vague memory of being a guest in their home and eating the handmade dumplings that were stuffed with meat and served with sour cream.

But I still don't know the joke that uncle Sava went to jail for. He never dared to share it with anyone.

The Truck That Came Too Late

At the start of the war, grandma Tsilia and her parents almost escaped.

Great-aunt Sabina, who was grandma Tsilia's younger sister, managed to hire a truck, hoping to pick up Tsilia and her parents and drive them to a railroad station, from where it was still possible to take the train east and escape deeper into Soviet territory.

But when the truck arrived, there was an air raid and grandma Tsilia and her parents hid somewhere, so the truck driver did not find them at their home address. The driver didn't have the time to wait, so he turned around and went back.

When my father was a little boy, he asked grandma why her family didn't run away from the Nazis. The Soviet Union was attacked on June 22, and Soroca wasn't occupied until almost a month later—on July 13. Why did they wait until the last minute? Why didn't they evacuate, like so many other people?

Grandma replied that they didn't flee because they believed that the Soviet Union was the most powerful nation in the world, that Germany would be defeated in just two or three weeks and then the war would be over.

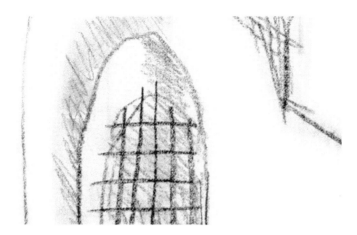

Expelled From Soroca

Before the war, so many Jews lived in Soroca that most streets had one or two synagogues. The central square was called "Synagogue Square" because there were eight synagogues in it.[16] When children played on the streets, they spoke Yiddish with each other—even non-Jewish children spoke Yiddish in Soroca.

Two weeks after the start of the war, when the Soviet army retreated, Jewish refugees flooded into Soroca from Balti and from Zguritsa. People wanted to get across the Dniester River to escape eastward together with the fleeing Russian Army, but very few managed to do so. To cross the fast-moving river, people stretched a rope from one bank to the other and when they pulled on the rope, a ferry moved across the water. But the day after Russian troops retreated (it was on July 7, 1941), two German airplanes bombed Soroca. At around noon, a bomb hit the cable that was used to ferry people across the river.

People went home, locked their doors, closed their window shutters and waited.

On July 13, the German army entered the town. When the Germans came into Soroca, two of their soldiers were killed. The Germans announced that they would murder forty Jews in retaliation. They went straight to the home of the chief rabbi of Soroca, whose name was Srul Ashkenazi, gave him a piece of paper, and ordered him to make a list of forty Jewish men to be executed. The rabbi took the paper and the pen, but only wrote one name on it—his own. The Nazis took him away. Then they went door-to-door in Soroca gathering forty-five men.

The chief rabbi and the forty-five Jewish men were taken outside of town and ordered to dig a grave. Then the Germans counted five men at random and let them go. They gunned down forty Jews and told the other five men to bury the dead. Then they told the five men to return home. That happened on July 15.

The next day, or maybe a few days later, the Germans announced that all the Jews had to come to the police station to register, and those who did not register would be killed.

It turned out to be a trap: after they were gathered in the Synagogue Square, the Nazis locked the Jews of Soroca in the synagogue for two days, without any food or water. Then they were forced, on foot, out of their hometown.

Vertujani

In the middle of July of 1941, the Jews of Soroca (I think my grandmother Tsilia with her parents might have been among them), were forced to walk 11 kilometers to Yampol. It took them all day. Then they were ordered to walk back to Soroca, where they were locked in the synagogue again. On the road, people drank river water and began to get sick from dysentery.

The Moldovans exchanged food for jewelry and clothes. A ring or a suit could get you a loaf of bread. Many Jews didn't have anything to exchange.

One survivor said that they stayed in the Yampol forest for a month, and that only about a thousand of the four thousand Jews who came into the forest survived.

Then they were marched for three more days without food or water and forced into a camp in Vertujani, where Jews from all over northern Moldova were gathered. It was a concentration camp that had barbed wire around it. As many as three hundred or four hundred people died there every day, especially because there was not enough water. There was a well, but there was not enough water in it for all the people in the camp. Jews waited in line for hours just to fill a kettle with water. There was a market where people exchanged their clothes for corn flour from the Moldovans, but the prisoners had to pay a "tax" to even go to this "market."

In the fall, when the rains started, the remaining Jews were forced on the road again.

"Had we stayed in Vertujani a couple more months, not one person would have been left," a survivor named German Belzer said[17].

The Frostbitten Feet

During the first winter in the Obodovka ghetto, my grandma Tsilia couldn't walk, because her feet were swollen and frostbitten so much that the tips of her toes broke off, my father told me. All she could do was lie on the ground. Her toes became frostbitten from sleeping outdoors in the forest while they were forced to walk barefoot to Ukraine. When she couldn't walk anymore, her father, Abram, carried her on his back. She was around 24 years old.

While listening to the testimonies of other survivors of the death march to the Obodovka camp, I heard a story about a Romanian commandant who did not allow the Jews to light fires to keep themselves warm at night when the temperatures fell below freezing. He said he would shoot anyone who tried to light a fire. In the morning, when the time came to continue walking, about twenty bodies remained on the ground[18].

Not every family was able to carry relatives who became too weak to walk.

Luckily, my grandmother was not abandoned on the road when she could no longer walk.

The German Wallet

In 1941, not long before he died, grandma Tsilia's father Abram was forced to work in a German hospital. One day, when the Germans were advancing further into the Soviet Union, they told him to do a final cleanup.

They didn't actually need the hospital to be cleaned, my father says, because they weren't going to come back there. But while sweeping the floor in one corner of the room, Abram found a wallet full of German money.

Grandma Tsilia told my father that she didn't think the Germans forgot the money, but left it there on purpose— as a tip, or maybe out of compassion. Maybe the wallet was left behind by accident, but it's remarkable to me that even in those terrible circumstances, my great-grandparents still believed that people had good intentions.

Still, during the winter of 1941, grandma Tsilia's mother, Perl, died. She died after eating some undercooked corn, grandma Tsilia remembered. They were boiling the grain, but she was so hungry that she could not wait for it to finish cooking and ate it raw.

After she died, her body was put into a mass grave, in a pile with other corpses. When he had some strength, Abram found his wife's body, and reburied her in a separate place. He didn't want her to be in one pit with all the other people, grandma Tsilia told my father.

Grandma Tsilia blamed herself for the death of her parents. She used to say that if her feet hadn't been frostbitten, if she had been able to walk, she would have been able to find some food to save her parents.

A Conversation

One evening I came home and my father was in a good mood. He wanted to talk. I said I didn't have time. I had a deadline. I had to write an article for work. I had to send it in before midnight.

"You should cherish every moment you have to talk to your father," my father said. "One day you won't have the chance anymore."

The Stolen Bread

One day in the ghetto, grandma Tsilia was lucky to get a loaf of bread. We don't know how she got this bread. When she returned home (if you can call the cowshed by that name), starving people surrounded her. Everyone was begging her for bread. She shared some with the others, but her father scolded her severely for this.

"How could you?!" he yelled. "We are dying from hunger and you are giving bread away!"

At night, she hid what remained of the bread under her head when she slept. When she awoke, the bread was gone. Someone had stolen it in the night.

Great-grandfather Abram grew weaker. One day, he fell while carrying water—people in the ghetto took turns bringing water into the cowshed. The next time when it was great-grandfather Abram's turn to bring water, he could not get up. Grandma Tsilia said that before he died, her father lost his mind and became aggressive; he recognized no one and let no one come near him.

He died on February 2, 1942. Grandma Tsilia remembered this date exactly because every year on the anniversary of his passing, she lit an oil lamp.

The Fake Email

When my father was 60 years old, he created a fake email address, and I stumbled on it once by accident when I was using his computer. It was a Gmail address for Abram Gelman.

I thought maybe my father used the fake email to do something secret—but when I logged into it, I saw that my father used the fake profile to play chess online.

I am not sure why my father wanted a fake name to play chess, and I don't know if my great-grandfather, who died before he turned 60, even knew how to play chess.

In any case, Abram Gelman never got to have a grave with his name engraved on stone. At least now he lives on in the virtual world.

Retaliation

My father remembers that grandmother Tsilia told him that there were two very cruel Jewish policemen in the ghetto. They forced the starving people to get up and go to work. The labor assignments included taking care of animals and bringing hay for them. The animals got food to eat, but the people got nothing. The Jewish policemen kicked my grandma Tsilia in the stomach to force her to get up. But she had frostbitten feet and could not walk.

These policemen were among the survivors when the war ended.

"What are their names? When I grow up I will find them and kill them!" my father told grandma Tsilia when he was little.

But when he grew up, he never tried to find them.

"I wonder where they are now. Probably they are dead," my father said, as he told us the story at the dinner table.

An Unexpected Meeting

One time when he was a little boy, my father went with grandma Tsilia to another town. On the street they ran into a man who hadn't seen grandma since the war. He was very surprised to meet her.

"Tsilia!" exclaimed the stranger. "You are alive!"

If that man was so surprised, my father thought when he was a little boy, then grandma Tsilia must have been in really sorry shape the last time he saw her in Obodovka. She must have looked like she was on her last legs.

A Love Story in the Ghetto?

According to my father's cousin Larisa, a German soldier saved grandma Tsilia's life in the ghetto. Larisa says she heard the story from her mother, who was grandma Tsilia's sister.

"It was a cold and rainy night when he smuggled her out of the ghetto, hiding her under his military coat," aunt Larisa told me on the phone when I called to ask about what she knows.

The reason that the German soldier—or it may have been a German medic—took her out of the ghetto is because he had overheard that there would be a so-called "clean-up" operation during which all the ill people who could not work would be killed, aunt Larisa said.

"Tsilia was so sick and so thin that he tied her body to his own, and that's how he carried her out of there," she said.

Tied her body to his?

"Yes, he was very much in love with her," aunt Larisa added. "I don't know what would have happened to her if he hadn't gotten her out of there."

After the German soldier carried my grandmother out of the camp, he arranged for her to stay with a Ukrainian family and brought food for her, Larisa said. He didn't forget about my grandmother even after the war ended. He wrote letters inquiring if she had survived. But by then she was already married to my grandfather.

When I heard the story about this German soldier, I thought that he should be the focus of my book. But what could I write? I knew nothing about him or about their love story.

All I can add is this: I remember my grandma Tsilia when she was in her seventies. She had skinny white fingers with blue veins that were visible through her thin skin. The skin on her hands reminded me of the skin on a dead chicken. She wore big glasses with thick lenses. I thought that she had strange habits, like collecting the unfinished food from dinner plates and putting it back into the pot for later. She had ugly feet. She spoke Russian with an accent and made grammatical mistakes. She would often repeat herself. When I was little, I remember thinking that I couldn't understand how anyone could fall in love with her.

But when she was young, grandma Tsilia was a very beautiful woman, Larisa said. Her eyes were green and sparkled in the sunlight. She was the kind of woman that you couldn't turn your gaze away from, people said.

Did Grandpa Know?

My father doesn't believe or doesn't want to believe the love story between grandma Tsilia and the German soldier. Maybe he doesn't like the idea of her being in a relationship with a German soldier. Of course, anyone who cooperated with the Nazis during the war could be seen as a traitor. Maybe my father is influenced by this thought as well. In any case, he says that we don't have the information firsthand. It's not from a primary source. Larisa may have embellished the truth.

My father won't let me ask grandpa Shlomo directly about grandma Tsilia's German soldier. He doesn't want to upset grandpa, in case he never knew about the soldier.

We agree, instead, for an indirect way to ask the question. "Were there Germans in the ghetto who helped the Jews?" I asked grandpa one day.

"Of course there were," grandpa Shlomo said, and looked away.

Then he changed the subject.

A few days later I tried again. I asked grandpa Shlomo, "Do you know how grandma Tsilia survived in the camp? Did anyone help her?"

Everyone always said that my grandma Tsilia was weak and sickly. When she was in the camp, she had frostbitten feet; she could barely walk. Her mother and father starved to death, leaving her on her own. How did it happen that she was one of the survivors?

But grandpa couldn't say anything about that. He didn't remember stories that other people told him about things that happened to them. He barely remembered the things that he lived through himself.

Or maybe he never knew anything about the German soldier because it was grandma's secret.

The Red Cross

I didn't want to make things up, so instead I started investigating. If the German soldier tried to find grandma after the war, he may have looked for her through the Red Cross. The Red Cross was how people looked for their lost loved ones after the war.

I contacted the Red Cross in Germany. They replied that they couldn't search for the German soldier directly without his name. But they said that they could search for my grandmother—to try to find out who may have been looking for her after the war.

The people at the German Red Cross were delighted to hear the story. I could tell from their emails that they really wanted to help. Of course, it must have made them feel good to look for a German man who saved a Jewish woman during the war. They sent me formal letters in the mail, addressed to "Frau Julie Masis." They wrote that my documents have been received and that they would inform me of the results of the search.

"Who are you hoping to find anyway?" my father said. "Even if you find his name, he would be around one hundred years old by now. He is probably dead."

Still, sometimes, I imagined meeting the children of the German man who saved my grandmother.

"What would you talk to them about?" my mother asked.

I would ask them to tell me the German soldier's side of the story. I am wondering if there is a family somewhere in Germany that has heard a grandfather's story about how he fell in love with a Jewish woman in a ghetto in Ukraine during the Second World War.

How Tsilia Met Shlomo

Because my father wouldn't let me ask grandpa Shlomo about the German soldier, I asked him to tell me the story about how he met my grandmother. It is a story that grandpa liked to tell.

They were in the same camp, but they didn't know each other. I think they must have met right before the liberation of Obodovka in 1944. Obodovka was liberated by the Red Army on March 15 of that year.

Grandpa Shlomo said that grandma Tsilia was looking for him. He was standing with five men, and she came and asked, "Which one of you is Shlomo?"

"Someone had told her about me, that I was a good man," grandpa Shlomo said. "She asked me what I did for work and then she asked if she could visit me at the place where I was living with my sister and my brother."

Grandpa must have liked her too because he invited her over. It was a cold day and they had to walk up some icy stairs. Grandpa Shlomo gave grandma Tsilia his hand. She exclaimed, "You have such warm hands!" The warmth of his hands swept her off her feet.

The Couple That Got Married in the Ghetto

One day, I received a Facebook message from Marina Blitshteyn, a woman from New York whose grandparents had also survived the Holocaust in Obodovka.

It turned out that like my grandparents, her grandparents, Motya Broytman and Luba Muchnik, also met in Obodovka. They even had a wedding party there.

"When they were getting married, they found some food for the wedding. I kept thinking—'How was it possible that they were able to scrape together enough food for a celebration?'" Blitshteyn said to me when we spoke on the phone.

Motya Broytman and Luba Muchnik were from the town of Edinets in Moldova—and like my grandparents, they walked home after being liberated. They followed just a step behind the advancing Soviet Army, so closely that they could hear the sound of gunfire in front of them.

When I heard this story, I wondered about how many other Jewish couples met in Obodovka—building new families after losing their parents, brothers and sisters.

How the Ghetto Was Liberated

While listening to the testimonies of Obodovka survivors using the USC Visual History Archive, I did not come across many stories about the day when Obodovka was liberated. Perhaps that day was somehow unremarkable, and that's why people did not remember it. But how could such a day have been unremarkable?

The only person who specifically talked about this day is survivor Petr Roitman. He said that Obodovka was liberated on March 14 of 1944. It was pouring rain, Roitman said. Soviet soldiers came with machine guns. The ghetto survivors told the soldiers where the policeman was staying and the soldiers went to his home and killed him, Roitman said.

"In the first few days, they killed anyone that we pointed at," Roitman said.

He estimated that fewer than a third of the Obodovka ghetto inmates survived.

One of the last Jews who was murdered in Obodovka was a 32-year-old tailor from Soroca named Froim Polyak. He was shot by the fascist troops as they retreated from the village, according to testimony that was submitted by his daughter to Yad Vashem. It is not clear whether those who murdered him were German or Romanian.

Romania's Responsibility

Some people say that Romanian fascists didn't murder Jews like the Germans because they didn't really accept Hitler's Final Solution.

According to grandma Tsilia, most of those who survived the first winter in Obodovka held out until liberation. Indeed, later in the course of the war, the Jews from the Obodovka camp began to receive assistance from the Romanian Jewish community, and a free canteen was set up. Perhaps seeing that the Germans were losing the war and worried about being held accountable, Romanian leader Ion Antonescu did not allow for the Jews on Romanian territory to be deported to death camps in Poland.

When I visited Ukraine, I heard stories about Jews who survived the Holocaust only because they escaped from German-occupied territory into territory that was under Romanian control.

For example, in Vinnitsa, Ukraine, which is only 140 kilometers from Obodovka, all the inhabitants of the ghetto were shot. There is a famous photograph called "The Last Jew of Vinnitsa" that depicts a bewildered Jewish man sitting at the edge of a pit full of corpses, with a soldier aiming a shotgun at the back of his head.

In parts of Ukraine under Romanian jurisdiction, the conditions were horrendous, but there was a chance to survive.

How My Grandparents Got Married

Grandpa Shlomo's brother Yasha, who was six years older, was also interested in Tsilia. One day, he went together with my grandpa Shlomo to meet her in an apartment that she shared with another girl in Obodovka—but on another visit, Yasha came alone. When she didn't see Shlomo, Tsilia asked, "Where is your brother?" When grandpa Shlomo tells this story, he laughs: "Tsilia liked me more than Yasha."

When Obodovka was liberated, grandma Tsilia and grandpa Shlomo walked back to their hometown in Moldova. They walked for many days, knocking on doors to spend the night. They were the first couple to register their marriage in Zguritsa after liberation, grandpa Shlomo said.

It was not an easy start to a married life. When he returned to Zguritsa, grandpa Shlomo found that his family home was destroyed. The roof was gone and one of the walls was missing. Grandpa told us that he traded his three-piece suit for a house across the street, because that house was in slightly better condition.

How Grandpa Got His Suit Back

"Have you heard the story about how grandpa got his suit back?" aunt Polina asked me one day, when I came over to my parents' house for Shabbat dinner.

"Was that after the war?" I asked.

"No, the war wasn't over yet," aunt Polina said. "It happened in 1944, after grandpa and grandma were liberated from the ghetto. They returned to Zguritsa, but they had nothing but the clothes on their back."

Right away grandpa Shlomo went to his neighbor's house, and asked the neighbor, "Do you know who stole all of our things?"

The Moldovans had looted Jewish homes and took whatever was left behind after all the Jews were kicked out of

Zguritsa because they didn't think the Jews would need any of their possessions anymore, my aunt said.

"Maybe the neighbor had taken some of the things himself too, but he didn't admit to it," aunt Polina said. "Instead he he said, 'Tell you what: On Sunday you go and wait near the church, and check to see if anyone comes to church wearing your clothes.'"

On Sundays, the Moldovans would get dressed up in their best clothes for church, aunt Polina clarified.

So the following Sunday grandpa waited outside the village church. Soon enough he saw a man wearing his striped blue suit from before the war.

"So did he get his suit back?" I asked.

"He did!" aunt Polina said. "He told the man that it was his suit, and he returned it."

The Bag That Took the Train

Soon after he returned home to Zguritsa, grandpa Shlomo was drafted into the Soviet Army. This was in 1944. Luckily, rather than sending him directly to the front, they first sent him to learn about radio transmission.

"They didn't trust me because I had lived under German occupation," grandpa Shlomo said.

One day, grandma Tsilia was on her way to visit grandpa Shlomo in the town of Nikolayev, where he was sent to study the Morse code, or whatever a telephone operator had to know. She was about to get on the train, but she had a heavy bag of food with her. She threw her bag into the train first, but at that very moment the train began moving and she didn't manage to climb in herself. She ran after the train, yelling to the passengers inside to throw her bag down. But they did not.

That day, grandma still had a little bit of money left, so she went to the market and bought two watermelons. She did not want to visit her husband empty-handed.

How Grandpa Killed Two Nazis

I always knew that grandpa Shlomo fought his way all the way to Prague, and then walked home to his village in Moldova—but that's about all I knew about his military service. He told us many stories about Obodovka, but he said almost nothing about the army.

When I asked, "Which was worse, the ghetto or the army?" he did not reply.

But recently, thanks to the Russian government's new online database that contains information on Red Army soldiers who fought in World War II, I discovered something about my grandfather's past that he never told anyone in the family about: that he killed two German soldiers during the war.

When I searched the site, I found a document that looked like it was typed in the 1940s. It said that my grandfather, as a telephone operator, "broke through enemy lines numerous times under heavy fire." And "in the battle for the city of Moravska Ostrava (in the Czech Republic), he repaired the communication line ten times, giving his commanders the ability to lead the battle without interruption. He killed two German soldiers with his personal weapon."

When we asked grandpa Shlomo about how he killed two Germans, he didn't deny it, but he did not tell us anything more about how it happened.

"I don't remember," he said. "It was a long time ago—more than seventy years ago."

Did grandpa Shlomo really forget how he killed two German soldiers, or did he just not want to talk about it?

How the War Ended

"Do you remember how the war ended, grandpa?" I asked one day, thinking, for some reason, that he would describe the day when he was liberated from the Obodovka ghetto.

But instead, grandpa remembered the actual end of the war: May 9, 1945.

In the afternoon when I asked him about the end of the war, we found him sitting outside on a bench, taking in the last rays of a summer evening. Aunt Polina had just left and now my father and I came to visit. Grandpa had a small bottle of water that he sipped from even though he was having a hard time swallowing. Sometimes he choked on the water and coughed. Then he would take another sip until all the water was gone.

"We were a night away from Berlin when we heard the announcement that the war ended," he said. "Everyone took off their hats and threw them to the ground. But they didn't let us go home right away. We had to cut down trees, to build wooden planks. It was another six months until they let us go."

Why did Soviet soldiers have to cut down trees to build something after the war, I wondered, but I didn't ask. Instead, I said, "Did they drive you home afterwards?"

"No, mostly we had to walk. Sometimes we got a ride for a part of the way, but mostly we walked. I was married by then, I had my wife and my sister and brother waiting for me at home."'

"Did you have a real wedding, grandpa?" I asked.

"No," he said. "We just invited a few people we knew and we announced to them that we were married."

"So, no white dress?"

"No, there was no white dress," he said.

Grandpa Shlomo's and grandma Tsilia's first child, Polina, was born in 1947. She was given a Russian name, Polina, but it was in honor of grandma Tsilia's mother, Perl, who died in Obodovka. My father came into the world ten years later. He was named after the two grandfathers he never met, because they starved to death in Obodovka. In the records, his name was registered as Saul, based on the first letters of his deceased grandfathers' names: grandpa Shlomo's father Srul and grandma Tsilia's father Abram (Avrum). It later became inconvenient for my father to have such a Jewish-sounding name, so he had it changed to Sasha (Alexander.)

Grandma Tsilia was 40 years old when my father was born and she thought she was too old to have a baby. When she found out that she was pregnant, she started thinking about getting an abortion, but grandpa Shlomo insisted that she keep the baby. He told her, "You just give birth, and I will raise the child."

My father with grandpa Shlomo

The Drive Home

One evening, my father said that grandpa was tired and I shouldn't ask him any more questions. When I heard my father say this, I felt guilty. I was questioning him, and I hadn't even told him that I was writing a book based on his memories. My father is the one who really loves grandpa, I thought; he cares about his well-being. And me, I mostly do it for my research. I am not saying that I don't love grandpa, but I think if I weren't writing this book, I wouldn't visit as often.

He has a big heart, my grandpa. Maybe it's because he is so close to death. When you are close to death, you pay attention to the things that matter the most, like love. But, in my defense, I should say that the more I got to know him, the more I cared about him.

That evening, grandpa got up and slowly shuffled back to his room, leaning on his walker, almost bending in two.

When we finally got to his room, I asked, "Was it scary to be in the army?"

"Of course," he said. "People died."

Then he added, unexpectedly, "I had a lot of good friends in the army, really nice Jewish guys."

"Did you keep in touch with them after the war?"

"No, they all went home, and I didn't hear from them again."

On the way home, as we drove on the highway, I asked my father, "Why did the army make grandpa build something from wood after the war?"

"Who knows," my father said, "You know, after Germany was defeated, the Soviet Union occupied Eastern Europe. It's not like they let all the soldiers go home right away."

Just then, a car swerved into our lane. My heart pounded at two hundred beats per minute. The seat belt tightened. And I thought that we could have died at this moment, and grandpa Shlomo would have outlived us.

PART THREE

GRANDDAUGHTER

I visited Zguritsa, Moldova, in 2015.

How I Was Named

When I was born, for a long time my parents didn't know what name to give me. I was nameless for weeks. They called me "the little mouse."

My grandfather Shlomo wanted to name me Sara, in honor of his mother. It is a Jewish custom to name babies after a family's ancestors. But who would name a girl Sara in the Soviet Union? There is no name that sounds more Jewish. To name a girl Sara was to set her up for humiliation and antisemitism.

So instead, my parents named me Yulia, a name they chose for no reason other than that they liked how it sounded. Yulia is not a Jewish name.

There had never been another Yulia in our family.

"Keep Moving, You Are Not a Tree!"

(Sept. 29, 2015, 10:42 a.m.) Arrived in Moscow. The flight to Ukraine is delayed, it will be here in seven hours. More time in Russia for me.

(Sept. 29, 2:20 p.m.) Messages over the loudspeakers at American airports: "Don't leave your bags unattended." Loudspeaker at the Moscow airport: "Please don't leave your children unattended!"

(Sept. 29, 4:48 p.m.) Advertisement in the airport café: "Bring food on board! Make your neighbor jealous!"

Making people jealous is good?

(Sept 29, 10:33 p.m.) Arrived in Odessa. It's scary. Men in military uniforms met our airplane, the airport has one tiny room—no restaurants, no ATM machine, dogs running across the baggage claim carousels. The streets are very dark. The taxi driver said they were better lit under the Soviets. The homes seem abandoned because there are no lights in the windows. The hotel, inside a totally unlit courtyard, had no sign on the door—for safety, explained the receptionist. But people are true to their reputation: very talkative and opinionated. And they get into long conversations with strangers.

(Sept. 30, 10 a.m.) The morning walk begins. I still have the same impression of a war-torn country. Breakfast: $2.50 for cherry-filled dumplings.

(Sept. 30, 4:17 p.m.) Odessa is so beautiful—cozy parks, old trees, a view of the blue sea below. Here are some festivals that take place in Odessa: Tomato Festival, Silent Film Festival, Baby Carriage Parade, International Beard Day, International Cat Show, and The Hairdressing Festival.

But Odessa has definitely seen better days, it seems. Buildings everywhere are deteriorating; many have boarded up windows and crumbling balconies. I saw a lot of elderly people digging through the trash or selling old clothes in the market. Very sad.

In the park, young men make money by inviting tourists to get their photo taken with an eagle.

A sign on many walls says: "Keep moving forward! You are not a tree!"

I tried to go into the synagogue on Jewish Street, but they didn't let me in because I was wearing jeans.

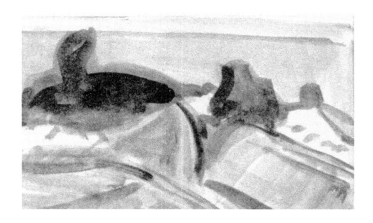

On the Road to Moldova

Between Odessa and the Moldovan border, our minibus rumbled along around huge potholes, the worst roads I've seen anywhere on the planet. Three times we were stopped by armed men who opened the doors and counted the passengers. These were Ukrainian military checkpoints. Our Moldovan driver blasted Russian and Romanian music. I took out my phone and recorded the songs that I liked. I looked out of the window and saw gray buildings under a gray sky, and women in high heels walking along dusty gray roads.

At the border, the Moldovan guard—it was a young woman—saw my American passport and called me over.

"Have you been to our country before?" she asked in Russian.

"Yes," I said uncertainly, for almost at that very moment it occurred to me that I had been to Moldova before. "But I don't remember anything because I was about five years old."

Actually, I do remember something about it: It was summertime, and there were rose gardens everywhere and walnut trees grew in rows along the roads. The landscape was hilly and beautiful.

"So why are you coming now?" the border guard persisted.

"My father is from Moldova," I said. "I wanted to see where he grew up."

I wondered if she thought that I was going to meet my long-lost father, whom I hadn't seen in thirty years. I always thought about this later, when I had to answer the same question. I often told people that I came to Moldova because that is where my father grew up, and I always wondered if they thought that I was half Moldovan. But my father is not ethnically Moldovan, but Jewish, and he barely knows the Moldovan language.

The border guard didn't ask me any more questions and only said, "Ok, I was just curious," and handed back my passport.

Our bus stopped at a shack that sold snacks. I only had American dollars, because there is no money exchange station at the Moldovan border with Ukraine. A man whom I didn't know offered to buy me a chocolate bar. It was the first example of Moldovan hospitality. All I could do was say thank you.

The toilet was across the road: an outhouse with a fence around it. I wasn't sure what the fence was there for, but Moldovans love their fences, especially brightly painted green ones. The toilet was just a hole in the ground, and there was no lock on the door. When I commented on the state of the facilities, the other passengers exclaimed, "Where did you come from? You should be thankful for this toilet." A woman I didn't know offered to hold my bag and make sure no one walked in while I crouched down to pee into the hole in the floor.

Why did I come to Moldova?

First, I wanted to visit Zguritsa, a former Jewish agricultural settlement that was home to my family for several generations. My father had been telling stories about Zguritsa ever since I was a little girl, but I had never seen the place. Also, I had a contract to write a story for The Jerusalem Post about a project to photograph every tombstone at every Jewish cemetery in Moldova. The Jews have mostly left this impoverished nation and the cemeteries are all that remains. Third, I had planned to take a trip to the village of Obodovka in Ukraine, where my grandparents survived the war and where my great-grandparents and great-uncles died.

Mostly, though, I decided to go to Moldova because I told myself that since I had lived for five years in Cambodia (a nation to which I had no connection), since I had traveled to Asia and South America—then I owed it to myself to see the places that my ancestors called home. I tried to convince my brother and my cousins to come with me, but everyone was busy. So when I saw a cheap one-way ticket to Ukraine, I just bought it.

Odessa is only a short bus ride from Moldova.

***

It was evening when I arrived in Balti, a city in northern Moldova not far from Zguritsa. My father arranged for me to stay in the home of his childhood friend, Shurik, whom he hadn't seen in more than thirty years.

Shurik lived in a Soviet-era building without an elevator. Soviet apartment blocks have many entrances, and after trying every wrong front door, I dragged my suitcase to the fifth floor and rang the bell, trying to catch my breath. Shurik's wife, Viorica, welcomed me in.

"Uncle Shurik is still at work," she said.

I followed her into the tiny kitchen as she warmed up some chicken soup with noodles. She spoke Russian with a Moldovan accent—it sounded like the accent that my grandmother had.

She gave me a towel and invited me to take a shower. I thought that it must be an Eastern European custom to bathe after traveling. It must be an old custom that goes back to a time when trips between cities took days, not hours. Or maybe she invited me to take a shower because she wanted me to take advantage of the fact that they had hot water. After the fall of the Soviet Union, the city of Balti stopped supplying hot water into apartment blocks. But Shurik set up his own water heater. Many people in Balti probably still don't have hot water at home, I thought, because hair salons all over town offer to wash people's hair for a small fee.

Shurik came from work with a cake in hand. He is a thin man in his late fifties with a very busy job. He is an obstetrician, and his patients are always phoning him when they have emergencies. In the 1990s, when Moldova was going through a tough time, the hospital where he worked ran out of surgical thread to stitch up women who had given birth. Apparently at that time they had to resort to non-medical materials for sewing up wounds. They used regular thread.

Shurik showed me a black and white photo he recently found in his album from his first day of school in Zguritsa, when he and my father were both seven years old. He told me a story about how he met my father in kindergarten: they sat at the same table and they were both lefties.

"Whenever we would switch the spoon from the right hand to the left hand, the teacher would yell at us," Shurik remembered.

The next day, Shurik and his twin brother, Vovka, drove me to Zguritsa.

A Visit to Zguritsa

My father told us many stories from Zguritsa, but I found that there was nothing particularly interesting about the village, nothing that might make a tourist want to take their camera out.

The house where my father grew up is no longer there. It collapsed years ago. Many houses in Zguritsa are unoccupied. Because of the poor economic situation in Moldova, nearly half of the population is now working overseas, especially in Italy. You don't get a sense of the emptiness in the Moldovan capital, but in Zguritsa, abandoned homes are everywhere.

There is a shallow river in Zguritsa, a creek with duck droppings along the banks. Shurik remembered that when he was little, he used to fish in this creek with his twin brother, Vovka.

Shurik said that he would walk in the water barefoot and eventually he would step on a fish. If you tried to bend over to pick up the little fish that you were standing on, you would get lighter and the fish would swim away from under your foot, he said.

A little downstream, Shurik brought me to the flour mill where grandpa Shlomo used to work. It is abandoned now, and it looks old, like it was built before the Second World War. I took a photo of a metal sign on the door because I wanted to see if grandpa Shlomo would recognize it. The sign says: "Be careful. Cigarettes and matches can start a fire."

Shurik stopped a horse-drawn wagon carrying vegetables and I got in for a ride. Horses are still used for transportation in rural Moldova. They are cheaper since they don't need gasoline.

Shurik told me that I must taste the water from the well because it is delicious. The well stands at the intersection of two roads, near a cross, and near the well there is a small clay container, into which water can be poured for the horses. I had a few sips of water from a metal bucket, but I don't remember anything about how it tasted.

We stopped to see my father's old school. It is now used as a storage for grain, guarded by a dog on a leash. Right near the school, I saw the old synagogue, a simple building with walls that are painted white. It's still locked just like it was when my father was little. I stood up on my tip-toes to peek into the window. There is nothing special about it, no frescos on the walls or on the ceiling.

My father's old classmate Radik, who is now a gym teacher in the new school in Zguritsa, recognized Shurik on the street and ran out to say hello.

"Shurik is that you?" he called out.

"And do you know who this is?" Shurik said as he pointed to me. "This is Sasha Masis's daughter."

Radik is the only one of my father's old classmates who still lives in Zguritsa. He looks fit and happy, but has a few missing teeth.

That day, I made a video on my phone about Zguritsa, and it got more than a thousand views on YouTube. I think the people who watched the video are the same people who used to live in all those abandoned homes.

Zguritsa Before the War

When my father was growing up in Zguritsa in the 1960s and the 1970s, there were no synagogues in the village—although before the war, there were several. My father didn't know that his village was once a Jewish settlement, where Yiddish-speaking residents made up 85 percent of the population. He didn't know that the public school where he studied in Russian was originally built as a Hebrew school by a Zionist organization. But he did know that the white building right next to the school, which was always locked and used to store grain, was once a synagogue. It was called "The Gates of Zion" and it was built at the beginning of the twentieth century.

According to census figures from 1930, Zguritsa had a population of about 3,000 people, of whom 2,500 were Jews.

Most of the residents were craftsmen—tailors, merchants, and shopkeepers. There were two synagogues—one for the wealthy, where the dues were higher, and a simpler one for those Jews who could not afford to contribute much.

At that time, the residents of Zguritsa did not celebrate birthdays, but they celebrated all the Jewish holidays and would not light fire on the Sabbath. Families kept a separate set of dishes in the attic for Passover. On Purim, villagers dressed in costumes and walked down the streets playing violins.

Theater troupes, Jewish singers, and performers visited Zguritsa on tour. Traveling actors performed plays by Sholem Aleichem. Visiting cantors sang in the synagogue, which wasn't large enough to accommodate everyone who wanted to hear them, so a crowd of people would always gather outside. There were no hotels, so the visiting actors were hosted in the homes of the villagers in exchange for free admission to the performances.[19]

In 1940, after the Soviet Union occupied Moldova, electricity came to the village. A radio was installed, and loudspeakers were put up on telephone poles. The villagers were amazed. "What a miracle," they marveled. "A bucket is hanging on a pole, and a human voice is coming out from it!."[20]

The Soviets also brought the cinema to Zguritsa. Movies were projected outdoors after sunset.

Today, all that is left of the Jewish community is the huge cemetery—it's so big that you can see no end to it. Some of our ancestors are buried there, my father says. One of them is grandpa Shlomo's grandfather, who died in the summer of 1916 just before grandpa Shlomo was born.

The Cow in the Cemetery

We approached the Jewish cemetery of Zguritsa cautiously, with sticks in hand. It is a large cemetery, one of the biggest Jewish cemeteries I've seen in Moldova. Someone had warned us that a pack of stray dogs live there. But instead of dogs, we saw a cow grazing near the entrance to the burial ground. Trying not to break any bones, we hopped from one destroyed headstone to the next.

"Can you read the inscriptions?" Shurik asked me.

I know the Hebrew alphabet, but I couldn't understand what was written on the stones. I wished I had someone with me who speaks Hebrew or Yiddish, I'd be curious to read the gravestones. All I could see is that many of the inscriptions started with the same phrase, but I had no idea what this phrase meant. We also came across sculptures of stone trees and tree stumps. Later I learned that the monuments of trees with broken branches were erected at Jewish cemeteries at the graves of children or anyone who left this world at a young age.

The cow wasn't in the cemetery just by chance. It seems that some villagers are transforming the Jewish cemetery into a pasture: the headstones in the middle of the cemetery have been moved aside to leave room for grass to grow.

Not a single Jew is left in Zguritsa today to look after the cemetery. I remember thinking that if all the Jews who have ancestors buried in Zguritsa donated some money, they would probably be able to hire someone to protect the cemetery. Someone would probably be happy to look after the cemetery for less than a hundred dollars per month. But as things stand now, no one is doing anything to preserve the burial ground.

Someone put up a sign on the road in Romanian and English with an arrow pointing to the cemetery. The sign says, "Ecotourism zone: Jewish cemetery, 'Spring of Life.'"

Why has the Jewish cemetery become an eco-tourism site? I guess maybe someone is hoping that it might bring more tourists like me to Zguritsa.

The Roma Capital of the World

It was a cold day in mid-October of 2015 when I visited Soroca.

Soroca is about twenty-five kilometers north of Zguritsa—it's a half-hour drive or a five-hour walk—and it is one of the most unusual places to visit in Moldova.

Soroca once had a large Jewish population (it was in Soroca that grandpa Shlomo found a shoe in 1941), but in recent years it became known as the Roma capital of the world.

If someone wants to see all of the world's most famous buildings in one place, they might want to save time and just come to Soroca. That's because the Roma people of Soroca try to outdo one another by turning their homes into the world's most famous architectural monuments. They built a replica of the US Congress, the St. Peter's Basilica and the Bolshoi Theatre. These are the mansions of the Gypsy kings on Gypsy Hill.

The town is also famous for its fifteenth-century fortress that stands on the banks of the Dniester River.

The fortress was locked when we arrived, but when Shurik knocked on the massive door, an elderly caretaker in a baseball cap appeared. He told us that he was about to go home, but if we really wanted to, he could wait a few minutes to let us see the fortress—for a small tip, we understood.

From the small dungeon windows of the fortress, we saw the patchwork of Ukrainian farms on the other side of the river.

But the Roma mansions of Soroca fascinated me more.

I knew that the Roma were also murdered during the Holocaust[3]. A few years later, I even interviewed the famous Roma Baron of Soroca, who told me that thanks to the negotiating skills of his great-grandfather, the Roma of Soroca were not deported to camps in Transnistria. [21]

---

3   Approximately 25,000 Roma were sent from Romania and Moldova to camps in Transnistria, from where only 11,000 people returned at the end of the war.

Like the Jews, the Roma perished in Transnistria from disease, starvation and cold. Romanian fascists were more lenient toward the Roma at first: While the Jews were deported from Moldova immediately after Romanian occupation began – in the summer of 1941 – the Roma were left alone until 1942. The Romanian army only deported the Roma whom they considered "unproductive" members of society – such as fortune-tellers, beggars and nomadic families. The Roma who were employed were usually not deported.

Later on, I reported for the Times of Israel about how the Moldovan Roma who survived the Holocaust received no financial compensation from Germany – unlike the Jewish survivors. I also wrote for Global Post about how the Roma Holocaust monument in Moldova had been destroyed by vandals.

I wanted to take a walk around Soroca to look at the Roma mansions, but it was starting to rain and Shurik was in a hurry to get back to Balti, where Viorica was waiting with dinner. Or maybe he didn't feel safe walking around there. There are so many rumors in Moldova about how the Gypsy kings became so rich.

After I came back to America, I asked grandpa Shlomo about the Gypsies—were they deported to camps in Transnistria together with the Jews? Were there Roma prisoners in the Obodovka ghetto?

But grandpa Shlomo said that he did not see the Roma during his time in Obodovka.

The Trip to Obodovka

No one in my family had gone back to visit Obodovka, where three of my great-grandparents, and one of my grandfather's brothers, Haim, lie in unmarked mass graves. I don't think anyone in the family ever even considered going there.

"What for?" my father said.

I guess it would be for the same reason that people visit cemeteries—to build a monument, to pray at the grave. But grandpa Shlomo and grandma Tsilia never wanted to see Obodovka again.

Since I was writing about Obodovka, I decided that I should go and see it, although I had no idea how to get there.

Luckily, when I was in Chisinau (the capital of Moldova), I interviewed a man whose job was to take photos of gravestones at Jewish cemeteries. Sergey is only a year older than me, and is passionately interested in history. When he isn't photographing cemeteries, he is looking for ancient coins in the forest with his metal detector or going on overnight trips with volunteers who are still searching for the remains of Red Army soldiers who went missing during WWII. More than seventy years later, soldiers are still being found. When I met him, Sergey had a very old car and a broken arm, the result of an injury in an overgrown Jewish cemetery. His arm needed surgery. But when I asked if he would be interested in going with me to Obodovka, he immediately agreed. Sergey is always up for a road trip, especially to see a place that has something to do with World War Two. When he agreed to drive me to Obodovka, he had only met me once.

Moldova is an ethnically divided nation—the Moldovans speak Romanian and want their country to be politically closer with Romania, and there are Russian speakers who lean more toward Russia politically. One of the points of division between the two ethnic groups is the Second World War. Ethnic Moldovans probably have mixed feelings about the war—when Romania, which sided with Hitler's Germany—fought with Soviet Russia. After all, it might seem better to be occupied by a country where the people speak the same language as you speak at home than to be ruled by Stalin, who sent millions to prison camps in Siberia.

Sergey is a Russian-speaking citizen of Moldova and is fiercely patriotic for all things Russian. He admires Vladimir Putin, and has great respect for Soviet soldiers who fought to liberate Moldova from Romanian occupation during the war. I think that is one reason why he volunteered to bring me to Obodovka.

We left Chisinau in the morning and drove on roads that were in such a bad state that in places the asphalt had worn off completely, and our car wobbled up and down on cobblestones that had been laid before cars existed.

We were fined as soon as we crossed the border into Transnistria because they have a law that vehicles have to keep their headlights on at all times, even in daytime. The fine was only four dollars.

When we arrived in Obodovka, it was early evening.

The first thing we saw when we drove into the village is a monument to another 20th century tragedy, Holodomor. This was a famine caused by Stalin's agricultural collectivization campaign that forced farmers to give away their grain to the government. At the entrance to Obodovka stands a huge cross that looks like a stalk of wheat, and the year 1933 is written across it. Just behind the cross in the woods, we saw graves marked by crosses. Some had names written on them, others were unnamed, holding the remains of many victims. Christian Orthodox cemeteries are different from Jewish ones. Ukrainians and Russians mark the graves with a wooden cross; Jews put a stone on the grave. Christian Orthodox cemeteries are often located in the forest, away from sight. Jewish cemeteries are usually on a hill overlooking a river - at least that's what I saw during my travels.

We drove around Obodovka looking for the place where the ghetto used to be. We picked up an elderly woman who was hitchhiking and gave her a ride down the road, and after she got into our car, we asked her to point us in the direction of the ghetto. We spoke to her in Russian and she understood us, but answered in Ukrainian. It seems that there is no public transportation in Obodovka, and the villagers, most of whom are elderly, get around by hitchhiking and riding bicycles even in the winter.

Like the rest of rural Ukraine, Obodovka looks like a place where the economy collapsed and never quite recovered. There used to be a communal farm in Obodovka that produced sugar beets, and there used to be a cattle farm—but when I visited in the fall of 2015 it looked like both were gone. I got the impression that all the young people left to look for work somewhere else, leaving the elderly to fend for themselves.

Following the directions of the villagers, we came to a clearing with a tall metal gate announcing the "Suvorov Kolhoz, a communal farm." A menorah stands in front of a concrete block that looks like it used to have a Soviet monument on it. The monument is gone, the communal farm is gone. All we saw was an empty parking lot. Sergey took out his camera and began taking pictures of the gate, he said it reminded him of the "Arbeit Macht Frei" sign at the entrances of Nazi concentration camps. He asked if I could sense anything unusual or ghostly. I felt nothing. We climbed over the gate, ignoring the "No Trespassing" sign. We found the brick foundations of a long building. Sergey said in all likelihood these were the foundations of the cowsheds because we saw cow bones scattered all over the ground. The bones made the place look like a cemetery or a mass execution site. There was no one around and it was quiet like in a cemetery.

Is this where the Obodovka ghetto was? Nothing was written on the menorah. This may have been the site of a massacre or this may have been the location of the ghetto. We were not sure that we found the right place.

The sun was setting, we were cold and hungry. Sergey wanted to drive to the next town, where I had reserved a hotel (there are no hotels in Obodovka), but I wanted to have dinner in Obodovka for symbolic reasons. The idea was to honor those Jews who had died from starvation here: the Nazis didn't kill us all.

There was no menu in the restaurant and we just asked them to bring us whatever they had. We ate sauerkraut with sunflower oil, borscht with bread, and cottage cheese dumplings. We didn't take off our coats and drank tea to warm up because there was no heat. It was only October and we were already freezing. How the Jews in the camp survived the winter without heat is beyond me.

There was also no heat in our hotel in Chechelnyk, which was disappointing, as I had imagined the entire evening how nice it would be once we got to our hotel and took a hot shower. There was also no hot water. The bathroom was at the end of a long hallway. The lady who worked at the hotel brought us extra blankets and a space heater. We paid for two rooms, but she said that there was only one space heater in the hotel. Sergey offered the heater to me, and took the blankets for himself.

In the morning, I was surprised to discover that the street outside our hotel no longer looked empty like it had the night before, but was swarming with people. Clad in black coats, dozens of people were selling their old clothes and shoes by laying them out on plastic bags on the ground.

We had breakfast in the downstairs cafe, which looked like a nightclub because it had floor to ceiling mirrors and swings instead of chairs. Customers could swing forward and back while sitting at their tables. We had tea and sandwiches and then we drove back to Obodovka because I wasn't convinced that we had seen everything that there was to see.

Once again, we asked passersby to show us the spot where the Jews were imprisoned during the war, and now someone pointed us to a different location. There we found several mounds that looked like graves and next to them a small monument, inscribed in Ukrainian, "To the men, the women, the elderly and the children who were ruthlessly murdered in the hours of Nazi occupation only because they were Jews. This must never happen again. The victims will be forever remembered."

I was happy to read this touching message. I am not sure who paid for the monument or who built it, but because it was written in Ukrainian, it seemed like it was a post-Soviet monument, either erected by the Ukrainians themselves, or for the Ukrainians.

But it was a generic monument. There was no information on it about the Obodovka ghetto. It could have said something like, "Ten thousand Moldovan Jews were imprisoned here between 1941 and 1944 by Romanian fascists. The ghetto was liberated on March 15, 1944"—but the monument gave no information. I later saw monuments with identical inscriptions at other Holocaust sites in Ukraine.

What I was thinking at the time is that it is unfortunate that, while there are Holocaust museums in practically every American city, on the very spot where thousands of people were murdered, there is practically nothing. There are no names of the victims, no plaque giving even the most basic information about what took place.

We wanted to speak to the villagers, and we thought about knocking on the door of a nearby home.

Just then an old man came walking on the road, and when Sergey approached him to ask some questions, he told us that he remembered the Jewish camp.

"The Jews were falling down from exhaustion. No one shot them, they were just collapsing and dying," he said. "And we threw food to them."

The old man said that he witnessed this when he was a child, and that his mother gave bread to the Jews.

I did not tell this man that I came to Obodovka because my great-grandparents were murdered there. I was always uncomfortable in Ukraine about revealing my Jewish identity.

A Classmate

Almost every survivor of the Obodovka camp whose video testimony I watched through the USC Visual History Archive said that he or she wouldn't have made it to the end of the war if it wasn't for help from the local Ukrainians.

One Jewish woman remembered that when she fell ill, a Ukrainian woman for whom she worked in Obodovka came into the camp and brought her milk.[22]

Some survivors recalled that Ukrainians used to bring food into the ghetto, even if it was for no one in particular. They would bring some beets and potatoes, and leave before anyone saw them.

One time, a Jewish boy from Obodovka who was imprisoned in the camp saw his Ukrainian classmate trying to do just that. Just as the Ukrainian boy approached the camp with the food that he brought, a German soldier saw him and shot him dead.[23]

"I saw it from a distance. I couldn't even tell his mother, because I could not leave the camp," said Petr Roitman, who survived the war. "Many Ukrainians helped and many were killed as a result."

The Righteous Among the Nations

The Yad Vashem Holocaust Remembrance Center in Israel has a database of the Righteous Among the Nations, which contains the names of non-Jewish people who risked their own lives to save their Jewish friends or neighbors.

It is also possible to search the database by location, and one day I typed "Obodovka" into the search to see what it would reveal. The search came up with only one family, Galina and Ivan Gudyma, who hid three Jews. Had I known about them, maybe I would have tried to find the Gudymas or their descendants when I visited Obodovka.

But the Gudymas were not the only Ukrainians in Obodovka who helped the Jews.

The names of those people who gave my grandfather bread and potatoes that he carried back to the starving people in the ghetto have been forgotten. The old man and the old woman who waited for him with breakfast every morning are not included on Yad Vashem's list of the righteous. And I also do not know the name of the German soldier who saved my grandmother's life.

Back in Odessa

(Nov. 19, 2015) Today I encountered antisemitism for the first time during my trip. It was in a conversation with a man in my hostel. We were discussing why old women look for things in the dumpster in Odessa. He said that it's not because they are poor, but more of a cultural phenomenon.

"It's a Jewish trait in the Odessa character, they just always want to get something for free," he said.

I didn't reply.

(Nov. 20–Nov. 26) I stayed with a Christian sect outside of Odessa for a few days. I ended up there because my cousin's wife put me in touch with someone Jewish she knew from Moldova, but it turned out that this man converted to Christianity. The sect members live together in one house and eat all their meals as a group and every time they go anywhere (to church or to the grocery store), they go all together in one van. They give all of their earnings to the leader of the group, whom they call "Uncle Vasya." They are all men except for one girl, Natasha, who cooks for everyone, but receives no salary. They have a traveling Christian choir. They have weekly Bible meetings. They have a garden. They also have a traditional Russian bathhouse as a side-business.

(Nov. 28) When they arrange to meet each other, people in Odessa set up their meetings outdoors, near famous monuments. I am supposed to meet a professor for an interview at 5 p.m., and he says, "Meet me near the Utesov statue." It's raining and it's freezing and it's windy, not to mention that it's dark. Why can't we meet in a café?

(Dec. 1) On the train to Chisinau I met a Moldovan woman who was getting ready to donate her kidney to a relative who needed a kidney transplant. She was going to travel to India for the surgery. After telling me her story, she took off her gold ring and tried to sell it to me. I didn't need a ring and had no cash on me.

The train conductor was drunk. When I asked him for a cup of tea, he grabbed my arm and said, "Are you sure that it's only tea that you want?"

There were no other young women on the train.

Kyiv, the Capital of Ukraine

I took the train to Kyiv. I stayed in the apartment of Natasha, a sister of my mother's friend.

(Dec. 21, 2015, 11:02 p.m.) Kyiv: Most people on the street speak Russian, but everything is written in Ukrainian. Street musicians sing in Russian, but in restaurants and cafes, there is no Russian music, only American Christmas carols. In the Russian drama theater, the repertoire is French, Spanish and English plays in Russian translation. There are no plays by Russian authors. It's as if Ukraine decided to boycott Russian music, Russian literature, and the Russian language. It seems to me that the official language is not the language that most people speak among themselves. Why don't multi-ethnic countries try bilingualism? I think it works so much better in Canada.

(Dec. 22) Natasha, my host in Kyiv, turns her Wi-Fi off at night because she is worried about radiation, she said. She also won't buy any fresh fruits or vegetables in winter because she says that they are probably grown in greenhouses with bad chemicals. Yet she is drinking the tap water in Kyiv, the city near Chernobyl that still doesn't allow people to burn tree leaves in the fall because doing so would release radioactive chemicals into the air. The level of radiation in Kyiv jumped from fifty microroentgens per hour before the nuclear accident to three thousand microroentgens per hour. Many of the radioactive substances have long half-lives and they will decay for many years. I find her fear of Wi-Fi and tomatoes quite ironic.

(Dec. 23) I asked Natasha what it was like to live here when Chernobyl exploded. She said all the cockroaches disappeared from the city and never returned, but the rats and the crows came back after two years. She said she got her children and her mother out of Kyiv as soon as she learned about the accident (about two days later), but nonetheless her son and her mother were both later diagnosed with a mild form of radiation sickness.

(Dec. 23) I visited Babi Yar, where my great-great grandfather on my mother's side was murdered during the war. I noticed how most of the memorials at Babi Yar have a faded or a stained area in the center. This is because they were vandalized with swastikas numerous times and then washed to get the swastikas to come off.

(Dec. 24) The one place where the Russian language officially remains in Ukraine, from what I've seen, is in the ATM machines. You can still take money out in Ukraine if you speak Russian.

(Dec. 25) I'm flying home on Christmas because that was the cheapest ticket I could get.

The Synagogue of Orhei

After I returned to the United States, I read in the news that the synagogue in Orhei, Moldova, was vandalized. The Torah scroll was thrown on the floor. In a photo, I saw a member of the Jewish community standing in disbelief in the trashed building.

"It makes me sad," I wrote to a friend in Moldova. "Because it shows that Moldovan people don't like Jews, that all my relatives were right when they left Moldova—because people don't like them, and they don't want them there."

"I don't know, maybe," he wrote back.

"Why don't people like the Jews?" I asked.

"It passes down from father to son," he replied. But a few months after the synagogue of Orhei was vandalized, the people of Orhei elected a Jewish mayor.

When they went to the polls, the residents of Orhei voted for Ilan Shor, a Moldovan Jew who was actually born in Israel.

"Why did people vote for him, even though he is Jewish?" I asked my Moldovan friend.

"What difference does it make that he is Jewish?" my friend replied.

Chisinau in the Summer

I traveled back to Moldova again a few months before grandpa celebrated his one hundredth birthday. It was summer. I rented a small apartment with a kitchen and a bedroom.

"How do you like Chisinau in the summer?" a friend asked in a Facebook message.

I wasn't sure what to say.

The mayor of the capital had been arrested because of a corruption charge. Four months later he was still under house arrest.

An arrest warrant had also been issued for the mayor of Moldova's second largest city, Balti, in connection to the attempted murder of a Russian banker, which he allegedly ordered. But the mayor of Orhei, Ilan Shor, who was sentenced to seven years in prison because of the billion that vanished from Moldova's banks, was still the mayor of Orhei.

I liked Chisinau: it was warm, the people were friendly, and fruits and vegetables were cheap and delicious. I went to the market and bought tomatoes, peaches, peppers and apricots—so many that I couldn't possibly eat them all.

When I came back from Moldova, grandpa Shlomo asked excitedly where I had been. He wanted to know which towns I visited—Chisinau, Edinets, Zguritsa, Balti, Chernivtsi—but even more, he wanted to know who I had met in Moldova. I wasn't sure who he wanted me to meet, but it seemed that he wanted to know if I met any of his old friends or neighbors, anyone who remembered him.

PART FOUR

AFTER THE WAR

Grandma Tsilia, my father's sister Polina, and grandpa Shlomo

The Famine of 1947

There was a famine in Moldova in 1947, the year when my aunt Polina was born. In our family they referred to this period as "golodovka"—"the year of hunger."

The only story I heard about it is that grandma Tsilia and grandpa Shlomo kept a bag of flour stashed away in the house to last them through the winter in case they ran out of food. Grandma would sometimes take a cup of flour out of this bag to bake something, and grandpa scolded her for it every time.

I assumed that this "year of hunger" must have been a minor thing—not the sort of hunger that they experienced in Obodovka, not a deadly hunger.

But when I did some research, I found out that there was a major famine in Moldova in 1947 caused by two years of drought and the collectivization of agriculture. According to some historians, five percent of Moldova's population perished that year, and in some villages in the south of the country nearly half of the residents starved to death. There were even cases of cannibalism.

Grandma Tsilia was 30 years old and pregnant in 1947. Somehow, despite everything, she gave birth to a healthy baby girl, my aunt Polina.

How a Poor Man Visited a Rich Man

According to my aunt Polina, grandma Tsilia loved to tell jokes. Whenever aunt Polina had her girlfriends over at her house when she was growing up in Zguritsa, grandma Tsilia would say, "I want to tell a joke," and then she would start telling it—even though aunt Polina had heard the same funny story many times, and did not want to hear it again.

"Do you remember a joke that grandma used to tell?" I asked.

"I used to, but I forgot," aunt Polina said, but then she remembered one.

It was a joke about a poor man who went over to a rich man's house. When the poor man knocked on the door, the rich man was having dinner—savoring delicious dumplings with cherries.

"Will you join me?" the rich man asked the poor man.

"No, thank you," the poor man replied politely.

"What?!" the rich man exclaimed. "Are you telling me that you are not hungry?"

And then the rich man ordered two of his servants to hold the visitor down and for the third servant to stuff dumplings into the poor man's mouth.

But the poor man began to scream.

"Wait a minute, let me find out why he is screaming," the rich man said to his servants.

"I want one man to hold me, and for two men to feed me," the poor man said.

This is not the funniest joke I ever heard, but I think it says something about the world my grandmother lived in. It was a world where poverty meant hunger, and wealth meant a surplus of food. Food was so important that even the jokes that people told were about food.

Potato Diplomacy

When grandpa Shlomo returned home after the war, he tried to grow potatoes on the same plot of land in Zguritsa where his family home stood before the war. The old house had been destroyed, but the land still belonged to our family. Grandpa planted potatoes on this plot, but every year when harvest time came, most of the potatoes were gone. Someone else dug them out of the ground first.

"Did the neighbors steal grandpa's potatoes?" I asked my father when he told the story.

"Who knows," my father said. "It could have been anyone."

Grandpa couldn't supervise the yard because it was a few streets away from his new home, my father said.

So one day grandpa made a deal with the neighbor whose house abutted the potato patch.

"Tell you what," he said to the neighbor, "You plant potatoes on my land and in the fall we can split the harvest."

The neighbor agreed, and ever since then grandpa got to harvest half of the potatoes, my father said.

"Wow! Grandpa came up with a solution! A win-win situation!" I said. "They should try something like that to solve the Israeli-Palestinian conflict.. instead of fighting over who the land belongs to."

"It won't work in Israel. It's a desert. Nothing grows over there," my father joked sadly.

The Free Cookies

The nursing home where grandpa Shlomo lives has free chocolate chip cookies in a basket near the front door. The cookies are individually wrapped in plastic, and next to them there is another basket with bananas.

I was hungry one day when I came to visit grandpa — so when I spotted the chocolate chip cookies in the basket, I took one.

But my father said, "I saw what you did! You stole a cookie!"

I thought he was joking. There was no sign next to the cookie basket with the words, "For nursing home patients only."

But my father wasn't joking.

When we got home, he said, "Those cookies are there for the seniors. You have a refrigerator at home, you can always open the fridge and see what's inside. But the people in the nursing home, if they get hungry between meals, all they have are those chocolate chip cookies. Those cookies are there for them, not for you."

I thought if the cookies ran out, the nursing home would just get more. The cost of cookies, compared with how much they spend on the nurses and medical equipment must be negligible. But I never took another chocolate chip cookie from the basket again.

Without His Grandparents

When my father was little, he didn't have any grandparents because they died in the ghetto.

"Can you imagine what it's like to grow up without your grandparents?" he said to me once, when we were in the car, on our way to visit grandpa Shlomo. "There was no one to tell me stories. There was no one to tell me about the history of our family."

When grandpa Shlomo and grandma Tsilia went to work, they left my father with the neighbors—because there were no relatives to babysit him.

"They would leave me by an elderly Jewish couple whose house was near ours," my father said. "But they were not our relatives, they were just strangers."

My father said that the reason he didn't learn to speak Yiddish or Hebrew is because he grew up without his grandparents.

"Our culture was lost," he said.

How the Horse Died

My father does not know his great-grandmother's name, but one strange story from her life passed down to him.

He remembered this story one Friday evening, as we lit Shabbat candles, and I asked if any of his grandparents or great-grandparents were religious or believed in God.

"Of course they were religious," my father said. "When they had problems, they always went to see their rabbi."

That's when he told me a story about grandma Tsilia's grandmother—the mother of her father, Abram Gelman—who once became very ill. She suffered from headaches and terrible nightmares. In her dreams, she saw that misfortune had befallen her family, that her children were ill and that she herself was on her deathbed. The dreams were so disturbing that the poor woman became afraid to go to sleep. (Maybe she was foreseeing the Holocaust?)

She went to see a Romanian doctor who prescribed some pills. But the headaches and the nightmares didn't go away.

Then she went to see the rabbi.

The rabbi asked, "Do you own any large animals?"

It had to be a large animal—for example a cat would not have been big enough, my father clarified, as he retold the story he heard from his mother.

My great-great-grandmother told the rabbi that they had a horse. The rabbi said a prayer, which was supposed to transfer all of my great-great-grandmother's illnesses to her horse.

A few days later, the horse died—and my great-great-grandmother stopped having headaches and bad dreams.

Yahrzeit

In the 1960s, when my father was little, the remaining Jews of Zguritsa continued to gather together to pray on the Yahrzeit, the annual commemoration of someone's death.

My father observed the Yahrzeit gatherings on February 2, which was the date when the grandfather he never met, Abram Gelman, died in Obodovka. Grandma Tsilia marked the anniversary of her father's death every year, but not her mother's death because she did not know the date when her mother died.

There was an old man with a white beard in Zguritsa who walked with a cane and was very poor. To earn his bread he collected bottles. He also had a part-time job gathering a minyan, or a quorum of ten Jews, for holidays and Yahrzeits.

He would knock on people's windows early in the morning with his cane to wake them up to go to someone's Yahrzeit, my father remembers. But although he looked exactly as my father imagined a Jew should look, this old man didn't know how to read the Hebrew prayers.

As everyone prayed in the living room, my father would listen from behind a door. They read from Jewish prayer books and one man sang, but my father didn't understand the words. When they finished praying, grandma Tsilia would serve herring, vodka and honey cake. Some of the visitors would tell grandma Tsilia that they remembered her father from before the war.

After my father turned 13, the age that marks adulthood for Jewish boys, he began being invited to pray with the other men. But he never learned to read Hebrew or to understand the words of the Jewish prayers.

"Grandpa Shlomo went to Hebrew school when he was small, but I didn't," my father said in his defense.

"Why didn't he teach you?" I asked.

"He was busy, he worked a lot."

But grandpa Shlomo said he didn't teach my father to read and write in Hebrew because the other Jews in Zguritsa didn't teach their children either.

"If they had taught their children, I would have done the same," grandpa said.

Childhood Games

My father had many friends when he was growing up in Zguritsa.

Tolik and Radik were Ukrainians, Marik was Jewish, Vova Gaina was Moldovan ("Gaina" means "chicken" in Romanian, so whenever the boys wanted to tease Vova, they would call him a rooster), and Shurik and Vova, who were twins, were Russian. All the boys lived within a two-minute walk of each other.

Some of the things they liked doing was stealing walnuts and rabbits from farms, going fishing at night, or sledding from a huge hill in the winter, holding onto one another to make a giant sled-train—and yelling at the top of their lungs when they were about to cross a street at full speed.

Whenever my mother listened to my father's stories about his childhood adventures, she got the sense that he must have had the best childhood anyone could have imagined.

But when they fought, the Zguritsa boys would yell racial slurs at each other. They were aware of each other's ethnicities. The Ukrainians and the Moldovans didn't like the Russians, and almost nobody liked the Jews. When his friends got angry at my father, they would yell "Dirty Jew!" at him. My father complained to grandpa Shlomo, and grandpa told him he should yell the word "Kuzist!" back at them. My father never knew what this word meant, but he yelled it back whenever his friends called him a Jew. The insult seemed effective: my father says his friends seemed like they got very offended when they heard this word.

When my father told me this story, I decided to look the word up. It turns out that it means a "fascist." The word comes from a neo-Nazi movement that existed in Romania during the 1930s.

Even though they played together, my father didn't go over to the homes of his Ukrainian and Moldovan friends, and they didn't come to his house either, he said.

The Blue Suit

One day, my father told me a story about a World War Two veteran from Zguritsa. May 9th was Victory Day in the Soviet Union. On this day there was always a big public celebration. Everyone would gather in the central park. The band played. The Jews celebrated too, because for them Victory Day was extra special.

The man in the blue suit would make the first speech because he was a Hero of the Soviet Union, the highest military honor that anyone could receive. On this day, everyone respected him and everyone offered to pour him a shot of vodka. Everyone wanted to drink with the hero.

"Come over here," people would call out to the man in the blue suit. "Let me fill your glass!"

The man in the blue suit couldn't say no.

My father remembers that when the celebration was over, the music stopped, and the sun was starting to set, you could go to the park and all you saw was empty bottles and candy wrappers everywhere. Everyone had gone home and only one man in his blue holiday suit with war medals was lying on the ground near the park fence.

One day, I asked my father to tell me more about this veteran.

"Oh, there is nothing special about that story," my father said.

"You must have thought it was special, otherwise you wouldn't have remembered it."

"The special thing about it is that it is ironic that someone who achieved something so great could fall so low," my father said.

"Was he the only alcoholic in Zguritsa?" I asked.

"No," my father laughed. "He was not the only alcoholic, but he was the only one who couldn't make it home. All the other alcoholics somehow found their way back home."

"Didn't he have a wife?" I asked.

"Yes, he was married. His daughter was in the same grade as me. His wife worked as a telephone operator at the post office," my father said.

"So why couldn't his wife get him from the park?" I asked.

"What could she do?" my father responded. "He was drunk and too heavy to lift, and she couldn't do anything. The best she could do is just let him sleep near the fence until morning, when he would wake up as fresh as a cucumber — that's a Russian expression.

"And what did he do to become a hero?" I asked.

"That I don't know," my father said. "All I remember is how he was lying there, passed out, with his holiday suit all covered in dirt."

Showing Disrespect

When my father was a boy, one day, he was playing with his friends and came across a German helmet on the ground in somebody's yard. This was probably in the 1960s.
"Look," one of my father's friends cried, "A Nazi helmet!"
   The boys went over to pick it up.
   That's when they heard a dog bark. The dog wasn't going to let anyone take away its bowl.

The Horse-Pulled Sleigh

One day at a New Year's Eve party, we were gathered around the table at my aunt's house, stuffing ourselves on traditional Russian holiday salads, and every dish seemed to have too much mayonnaise. The year of the dragon was starting, and to mark the occasion I had put on a colorful dress made from Chinese silk. It hadn't snowed at all this winter, so my father began to reminisce about how cold winters used to be in Moldova when he was growing up.

In those days, fifty years ago, there was so much snow on the ground that in the wintertime Moldovan peasants exchanged their horse-drawn carriages for horse-pulled sleighs, he said.

One winter day, when he was little, my father had to return to Zguritsa from another village which was about ten kilometers away. There was a snowstorm that day and grandpa Shlomo hired a sleigh to bring my father home.

The sleigh moved slowly along the snowy road, and the ten kilometers seemed to stretch forever. After a while my father became so cold that he couldn't feel his feet.

"I'm freezing," he complained to the driver.

"And you know what the driver said to me?" my father asked as he told the story. "He told me to climb down and run behind the sleigh, holding on with one hand. So I trotted behind the horse all the way to Zguritsa."

"When I got home, I went directly to the stove to warm up, and I told grandma Tsilia that if I had stayed out there any longer, my feet would have been as frostbitten as hers were during the war."

Antisemitism

One day, when my father was about 14 years old, a child shouted something antisemitic at him.

My father reacted to the insult with violence: he punched the boy in the stomach.

A few days later, the boy's mother came to complain to my father's parents. She said, "Your son beat up my boy!"

But my father said to her, "Your son insulted me, and if he insults me again, I will hit him again!"

A few days or weeks later, the boy's older brother returned to Zguritsa. He and his buddies caught my father, held his arms and legs down, and tried to stuff soil into his mouth. They wanted to make him eat dirt.

"Too bad Hitler didn't kill all of you!" they shouted.

My father fought his way free and ran away.

Maybe that's when he began thinking about leaving the Soviet Union. He felt that he didn't belong in the country where he was born.

The Man who Wanted to Make My Father Blind

The worst incident of antisemitism in my father's childhood almost cost him his eyesight.

"The mean things that people said to me hurt my feelings, but those things were just words," my father began. "People told me to get out of the country and go back to Israel. I was hurt when they said that to me, because Moldova was my home, and I had never been to Israel. But another thing altogether was the violence."

The worst incident of antisemitism took place when he was about ten years old, he said.

One day, a man in Zguritsa was cutting some metal with a machine, and he asked my father to come and help him. "I can't see anything through this mask," the man told my father. "Would you come here and look where I'm cutting, so that I cut in a straight line?"

My father did so, but after looking at the very bright sparks from the metal cutter, everything went white in his vision and he could barely see anything. Somehow he found his way home, and luckily the incident didn't damage his eyesight permanently.

"Maybe he didn't do it on purpose?" I asked my father when I heard the story. "Maybe he was just stupid, or he didn't realize what he was doing?"

"There is no doubt in my mind that he did it on purpose," my father said.

The Only Man in Zguritsa Who Had a Car

One day, my father told us a story about the only man in Zguritsa who owned a car.

This story resurfaced in my father's memory when he was taking his daily walk in our neighborhood one summer afternoon.

This unlucky car owner from my father's childhood owned a Zaporozhets. The Zaporozhets was a cheap Soviet car model and the government gave away some of these cars for free to people who were handicapped or couldn't walk, my father said.

This car wasn't anyone's dream vehicle because it was small and slow. The only advantage it offered is that its engine was in the back (where the trunk is normally located), which made it better at driving through mud without getting stuck, according to my father.

One day back in Zguritsa, a boy was riding a motorcycle recklessly down the hill, when a truck drove up behind him.

"You know that metal running board that Soviet trucks had near the driver's cabin?" my father continued, as he told the story to my mother. "It sliced his leg right off."

"Oh my God!" my mother exclaimed.

When this handicapped boy grew up, he received a Zaporozhets from the Soviet government, and became the only person in Zguritsa to own a car.

One day, my father missed his bus home from Soroca, where grandpa Shlomo sent him for music lessons. Just then, he spotted a red Zaporozhets driving down the road. He instantly knew who the car belonged to. Hoping for a lift home, my father ran and caught up with the Zaporojets (that's how slow it was—you could actually catch up to it by running), and knocked on the car roof.

"The Zaporozhets was really low to the ground, so it was easy to reach the roof," my father clarified.

But instead of stopping to pick him up, the driver sped away. "The next time I ran into that guy's mother, I told her that I saw her son in Soroca," my father continued, "and that I knocked on his car roof because I wanted a ride home, but he didn't pick me up."

"And you know what she said?" my father continued, and my mother and I were all ears.

"So it was you!" his mother exclaimed. My son told me that he was driving down the road, minding his own business, when some antisemites started throwing rocks at his car."

"So that's how rumors start!" my mother laughed.

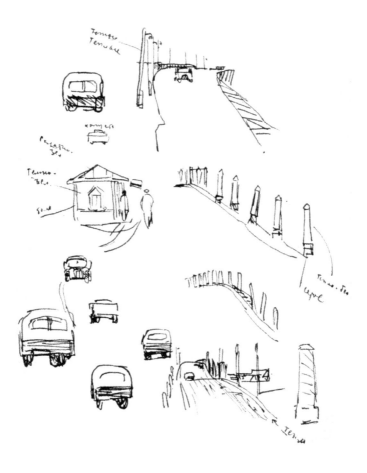

How a Tobacco Factory Cured Grandpa

Whenever grandpa Shlomo would start to talk about the war and about Obodovka, grandma Tsilia would ask him to stop. "Don't talk about it in front of the children, don't even think about it!" grandma Tsilia would say to him.

You might think that grandpa Shlomo is an optimist. Half of the Jews in the Obodovka ghetto died during the first winter. Corpses lay in a pile in the cowshed because people were too exhausted to dig graves. But whenever grandpa Shlomo talks about Obodovka, he doesn't mention death. He talks about saving his brother, and about the good people who helped him to survive.

Yet many years after the end of the war, grandpa Shlomo became depressed. It happened after he lost his job. According to my father, grandpa Shlomo was used to working 16 hours per day, six days per week. He left home at six in the morning and didn't return until 11 at night. When he came home for lunch, he would doze off on the couch with a newspaper on his face for about a half hour before going back to work. He'd close his eyes and instantly begin snoring. That's how tired he was, my father says.

But after grandpa was fired from his job, he became so depressed that he would refuse to get up from his bed in the morning. He just lay in bed all day, no matter how much grandma Tsilia tried to get him up. Eventually, she brought grandpa Shlomo to a doctor and the doctor gave him a prescription for lithium, which is an antidepressant.

My father says that grandpa's depression ended after he found a new job. It was at a tobacco plant, and he had to carry sacks loaded with tobacco on his back. Yet just a few days after he started working again, grandpa Shlomo's depression vanished.

The job cured him, my father says.

Or maybe it was the lithium. He continued taking lithium all of his life.

The Antenna

Around the time when grandpa was fired from his job, my father was learning about how antennas work and how they can capture waves from hundreds of kilometers away. So he decided to build his own antenna to watch television from across the border in Romania.

Nowadays, anyone in Moldova can buy a bus ticket and be in Iasi or in Bucharest a few hours later, but back then the borders of the Soviet Union were sealed and people felt like they were locked in. Naturally, they thought that everything that was interesting was happening on the other side of the border.

After my father built his antenna, he tried to set it up on the roof, which was no easy task. He was just a skinny boy back then. So he went to grandpa Shlomo for help.

"Help me get the antenna on the roof, papa," he asked.

But grandpa was lying in bed and not interested in anything because he was depressed.

"What for?" he said.

"So we can see Romania."

"What for?" grandpa said.

"It will be interesting!" my father said.

"Doesn't sound interesting to me," grandpa said, and turned to face the wall.

Then my father went to grandma Tsilia.

"I can't get the antenna on the roof," he complained to her. "And dad doesn't want to help me."

At that time, it was a daily struggle for grandma Tsilia to force grandpa Shlomo out of bed.

"Get up!" she shouted at her husband.

"What for?" grandpa said.

"Go help your son set the antenna up on the roof," she said.

So grandpa eventually got up, and helped my father to set up the antenna.

"So did it work? What did you see?" I asked my father when he told the story.

"We saw some TV channels from Romania."

"But you don't even speak Romanian," I said.

"That didn't matter," my father said. "What mattered is that everyone in Zguritsa began talking about how our home had an antenna on the roof and that we could watch Romanian channels on TV."

"Anyway," my father continued, "When grandpa Shlomo and grandma Tsilia were selling their house in Zguritsa before they came to America, all the Moldovans wanted to buy it because of that antenna."

The Most Important Thing in Life

My parents met at a Jewish holiday party when they were about 20 years old. Neither of them was particularly religious, and it was probably the first time my mother attended a Jewish social event. It was in the fall. It might have been Simchat Torah, my mother says, which in 1978 fell on October 24.

My mother spotted my father, but she also saw that he came to the party with another girl. Still, even though he was there with another girl, my father asked my mother to dance. They liked each other, but when my mother left the party that night, my father forgot to ask for her phone number. All he remembered was her first name: Dina.

The next morning, when my father woke up, his first thought was about the girl he met at the party. How could he see her again? So he called everyone he knew who had been at the party, and asked them for the phone numbers of everyone else whom they knew. Finally, he reached the only person who knew my mother at the party.

Four months after my parents met, my father got into a serious car accident while riding in a taxi. His driver and a passenger in the other car were killed. Bleeding from a wound in his head, my father was rushed to the closest medical facility, which happened to be a maternity hospital. The ambulance that brought him was almost turned away because it was the wrong kind of hospital for a car accident. Luckily the doctor who was on duty took pity on the young man. My father remembers that as women were screaming in childbirth, he felt ecstatic at the pain of the doctor's needle piercing his skin. The doctor stitched his wound. The needle reassured my father that he would not die.

In the moments after the accident, my father says his whole life flashed before him. Thoughts that had preoccupied him just a few minutes prior became irrelevant. At that moment, he said, he realized the most important thing in his life.

"What was it?" I asked when he told the story.

"What do you think?" he said, responding to my question with a question.

"I know," I said, thinking back to the time when I thought I was going to die in a plane crash. "The most important thing is to tell people that you love them and to forgive and ask to be forgiven."

"Yes," my father said quietly. "The most important thing was my love for Dina."

A few months after my father almost died, my parents got married.

The Matchmaker

Grandpa Shlomo came late to my parents' wedding.

My mother and father remember, to this day, that they worried he wasn't going to show up at all. By the time he arrived, the ceremony was over, and the bride and groom—actually, they were already husband and wife—were getting into their taxi. It was raining. Grandpa Shlomo arrived just in time to get his photo taken under someone's umbrella.

My parents still wonder what he was up to the morning of their wedding, what sort of business he had to take care of in Leningrad that caused him to be late.

Actually grandpa Shlomo takes weddings very seriously because that's all he ever talks to me about.

"Do you see the way I am now?" he whispered to me when I visited him in the nursing home around the time when he was 99 years old.

"Yes, grandpa, I see you," I said.

"I am now behind the times, I am not the man that I used to be," he said. "If I was still the same man as before, I would find a husband for you, I would."

Then he paused and whispered proudly, "I used to find husbands for everyone!"

For whom exactly grandpa found husbands I didn't have time to ask. According to my father, though, he found a husband for aunt Polina, after he realized that the boy she was dating played cards for money.

One day aunt Polina told grandpa Shlomo that her boyfriend won a thousand rubles in a card game. This was a huge sum in the Soviet Union, where the average salary was a little more than a hundred rubles per month.

But grandpa Shlomo said: "Go and tell him to give the money back—and if he does that, then you can go out with him a few more times and see how it goes. But if he does not return the money, you should break up with him."

A marriage with a gambler would not be a good choice for Polina, grandpa Shlomo reasoned, so he worked his connections until he found Peter, who later became Polina's husband.

"Who else did grandpa Shlomo find husbands for?" I asked my father.

"How should I know? He didn't find a husband for me," my father answered with his typical sarcasm.

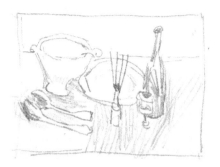

Grandma's Letters

After my parents got married, grandma Tsilia used to write them letters. It was a time when long-distance phone calls in the Soviet Union required a trip to the post office. So instead grandma Tsilia wrote letters and mailed them from Moldova to Leningrad, where my parents lived. The reason my parents saved the letters is because grandma included her recipes in them—my father's favorite foods that she wanted my mother to learn to cook.

She wrote down the recipes for her potato knishes, and a honey cake that my father loved from childhood. Her recipes were Jewish recipes from Romania and Moldova, the recipes that grandma probably learned from her mother. Grandma

Tsilia wrote that it gave her great pleasure to know that my mother would make something based on her instructions.

I only read one of her recipes once, maybe because I felt like I had no right to read the letters that were not addressed to me, even 30 years later. The letter began with the greeting, "My dear children,"— grandma Tsilia always addressed her letters to both my mother and my father together—and it mentioned that grandpa Shlomo was sending my parents a box of walnuts, still in their shells, and some honey. She urged my parents to eat well, and to not try to save money on food.

"Good health is the most important thing," she advised.

After grandma Tsilia died, my father scanned her letters and organized them carefully on his computer. Maybe now her recipes will live on for future generations.

How My Father Got Arrested in the Cinema

After my father got married, he worked the night shift at a textile factory. He had a university degree in textile production, so he wasn't just an ordinary factory worker, but a supervisor overlooking the work of others, mostly women.

During those years, my father used to come home from the factory in the morning when everyone else was just getting ready to go to work. He would go to sleep in the morning and wake up in the late afternoon.

On one of those afternoons, he decided to go to the movies. He had a few hours left before he had to go back to work.

"Just because I work the night shift, doesn't mean I can't ever see a movie," he thought to himself.

So he went by himself to the cinema and bought a ticket to an afternoon screening of some Soviet war film. The theater was mostly empty at that time of the day.

But my father never got to see the end of that movie. Suddenly the lights came on and police began to question everyone in the theater. Being unemployed and going to the movies in the middle of the workday was practically a criminal offense in the Soviet Union, it was called "tuneyadstvo." "Tuneyadstvo"—is one of those words that I don't know how to translate to English. It means something like being a parasite, mooching off society. Just like truancy, or cutting school, is an offense for which we punish students in high school, in the USSR, going to the movies on a workday without a valid excuse was something that could get a person in trouble.

A policeman came over to my father and said, "Let's see your documents!" But my father could show him nothing because he didn't bring his passport to the movie theater. So the policeman told him to get into the police van because they were going to arrest him.

"If they didn't want people going to the movies in the afternoon, why wouldn't they just close the movie theater?" my father remarked as he told the story.

When he was in the police van, my father managed to convince the police that he worked the night shift at the textile factory, and they eventually believed him and let him go.

"So did you get your money back for the movie ticket?" I asked.

He laughed.

"Of course not! This was the Soviet Union!" he said. "I was just happy that they let me go!"

How My Father Sent Butter in the Mail

In the early 1990s, when the Soviet Union collapsed, the Russian government introduced food ration cards. The first card they introduced was for vodka—it limited how many bottles a person could buy in a month.

"As if vodka was the most important food," my father laughed when he remembered this. "We never drank vodka, but once the ration cards were introduced, we felt that we had to stock up. We couldn't let the coupons go to waste."

Then the ration cards for other items were added, too: butter, sugar, meat. By the time we left in 1992, there were food rations for just about everything, my father said.

I remember the fear and panic I perceived in my grandparents' small kitchen when the rations for sugar appeared. Food in Leningrad hadn't been rationed since the Second World War. The elderly people still remembered the Nazi siege when a million of the city's residents died from starvation. Maybe it was then that my grandfather told my parents it was time to leave the country.

Still, while food was limited in Leningrad, in more remote parts of the former Soviet Union the situation was even more dire. One time, my father spoke on the phone with grandma Tsilia and found out that butter had vanished from the grocery stores in Moldova.

"Bread won't go down without butter. It gets stuck in the throat," grandma Tsilia complained to my father when they spoke.

So my father devised a way to mail butter from Saint-Petersburg (by that time Leningrad was renamed). Parcels took ten days to travel to Moldova by mail. To make sure that the butter didn't spoil, my father purchased a chunk of dry ice from an ice-cream saleswoman.

"They didn't use refrigerators in their ice-cream carts. They used dry ice. You had to wear gloves when handling it or you'd get burned," my father said.

He cut out a Styrofoam box, into which he placed the butter and the dry ice. The scheme worked. By the time grandma Tsilia received the parcel ten days later, the butter hadn't even melted.

"I saved my parents," my father said proudly, when he retold this story many years later.

The Hospital on the Way to America

When my parents got married, my father told my mother's parents that he dreamed about going to America and bringing my mother with him. But my grandfather Simon, my mother's father, said: "Only over my dead body."

But in 1991, when the Soviet Union fell and the economy collapsed, and beggars and racist marchers appeared in the streets, my grandparents told my father, "If you still want to go to America, you can go."

My father applied for visas to countries all over the world: Australia, Canada, even South Africa. Finally, because he had cousins in Boston, the United States accepted us. But a medical exam was required because Americans didn't want immigrants bringing in any contagious diseases. The American Embassy organized medical exams in Moscow, and we had to go there by train from Saint-Petersburg.

I remember a very crowded building. There were children and elderly people there, but there were no chairs, and no food or water. We had to stand and wait for many hours. People were tired and angry. But the medical exam may have saved my mother's life because doctors noticed something unusual on her chest X-ray. It turned out to be tuberculosis.

Our departure from Russia was delayed by a year while my mother was treated in a tuberculosis hospital.

Tuberculosis is a disease that affects particularly the poor in crowded conditions, it is especially prevalent in prison. Some patients in the tuberculosis hospital where my mother spent many months looked like they just got out of prison, my mother says.

My mother says she learned a very important lesson in that hospital—and it had nothing to do with disease. It was simply that she realized that she could make friends with everyone—even with former prisoners, with prostitutes, with those who were uneducated or unlucky. She realized that you can relate to everyone when you share a deadly disease.

A year later my mother recovered, and my parents sold their car and their furniture, and packed bed sheets, clothes, cups and plates, Russian books and old family photographs into huge travel bags. Now that I think of it, I don't understand why it was necessary to bring so much stuff.

My mom brought her tuberculosis medications along with her because she thought throwing the pills away might jinx her.

Before we left Leningrad, I remember having a liberating feeling that I didn't have to do my homework or even go to school—because we were leaving and never coming back. But I also remember a nightmare I had one night that I was living in a broken-down house with a leaky roof. (I think this dream might be a premonition about the poverty that awaits in my old age.)

On our last day in Leningrad, my maternal grandmother sobbed that she would never see us again. She said she was old and she would die before she would have a chance to visit us.

When I saw her crying, I started to cry too.

How We Came to America

I was ten years old when we flew to America with my father's parents, grandpa Shlomo and grandma Tsilia, who were in their seventies. I didn't grow up with them. They lived far from us in Moldova, spoke with an accent, and had strange, non-Russian names, I thought. I was much closer with my mother's parents.

Our flight was delayed and we had to spend the night in the airport, sleeping on the floor like refugees. My parents had sold everything and exchanged their Russian rubles for American dollars, so they couldn't bear to spend the meager cash for food in the overpriced airport. I remember that we all scraped in our pockets for the Russian coins that remained and managed to buy some tea and cookies.

It was my first time in an airplane, but I was not afraid to fly back then the way I am afraid to fly now. It didn't occur to me that this machine that was built by adults could malfunction. But grandma Tsilia was disoriented. My parents said that during the flight she felt suffocated and asked the crew to open a window or to let her step outside to take a breath of fresh air.

America wasn't as we had imagined. Instead of sky-scrappers, people lived in private homes, the kinds of buildings that you didn't see in Russian urban centers.

My mother soon found a job in another state, where she rented a small studio apartment and visited us only on weekends. Grandpa Shlomo and my eight-year-old brother, Boris, used to walk the streets picking up furniture or appliances that someone threw away. When I wasn't in school (where I had to learn to open plastic packages and eat brightly colored things that didn't look like food), I was sent to a dentist who put fillings into every single one of my teeth, fillings that I didn't need.

During the summer, my parents signed me up for a Jewish summer camp. It had a swimming pool, where I almost drowned because I barely knew how to swim. It was my first time in a summer camp, and my first time in a place where everyone around me was Jewish. Despite the tennis lessons, the arts and crafts, and the dance class, which I liked—being sent to a "Jewish camp" made me very uncomfortable. I had never been to a place were Jews were segregated from others. The only Jewish camp I had heard about before was the camp in Obodovka.

How Grandpa Got Lost

The first day after we came to America, when everyone else was sleeping off the jet lag, grandpa Shlomo went exploring. At least my father insists that it happened on the very first day after we arrived in Lynn, Massachusetts (which is a suburb of Boston)—but my mother says it probably happened during the first week. It was in January of 1992 and grandpa Shlomo was 75 years old.

"When everyone woke up from their afternoon nap, he was just gone," my father says. "No one knew where he went."

Grandpa Shlomo decided to go see what was around—and the first place he wanted to check out was the market, naturally. So he asked someone how to get to the market and someone actually understood him because there were many Russian immigrants living in Lynn then. That was how he got on the bus and rode to Haymarket, the biggest outdoor market in Boston.

Finding the way back to Lynn proved more difficult. Grandpa tried to speak Russian, but no one understood him. He tried in Yiddish, and he tried in Romanian—and still no one understood.

Finally, he just got on a random bus, but ended up in some other town. When he realized that he was not in the right city, grandpa didn't get off the bus, but just rode around all day, until it got dark and the bus driver's shift finished. All he could say to the bus driver was the word "Lynn."

Finally the bus driver felt sorry for him, and drove him back to Lynn in an empty bus, my father says.

"What kind of place did you bring me to?" grandpa Shlomo asked my father that evening. "I speak four languages and no one understands me!"

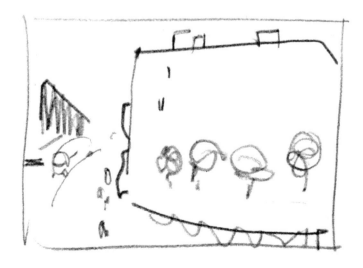

Grandpa's Trip to Israel

When grandpa Shlomo was about 80 years old, his lifelong dream came true and he finally got to go to Israel. He went on his own and stayed for about a month, visiting cousins and friends from Moldova, some of whom he hadn't seen in decades. He also visited the graves of his friends from Zguritsa. He dressed up in his suit and tie and got his picture taken in front of the Western Wall.

"Weren't you worried about letting grandpa travel so far away on his own?" I asked my father.

"Not at all!" my father said. "Grandpa was very independent until he was about ninety-five years old."

Why Grandpa Didn't Learn to Drive

When grandpa came to America, he wanted to get a driver's license, even though he had never driven a car in his life.

"Do you think I should get a driver's license?" he asked my father one day.

"What are you talking about? You are too old to drive," my father told him.

Years later my father realized that he was wrong. He said that if he had known that grandpa was going to live for another 25 years, he would have encouraged him to learn to drive.

Why Grandpa Didn't Remarry

A few years after grandma Tsilia died, grandpa Shlomo met a lady that he liked. He asked my father if he should get remarried. The lady was a widow, and my grandpa was a widower; both of them were probably around 80 years old then.

But my father discouraged him, "It doesn't make sense to get married at your age. You are too old," he said.

Grandpa's Sunglasses

The last time I visited, grandpa Shlomo gave me a pair of old sunglasses. He found them in his desk drawer and decided to make a gift for me.

"I love you because you come to visit me," he said, as he gave me the sunglasses.

I put the glasses on carefully (the lenses had greasy fingerprints on them), and bent over to gaze into the small mirror on grandpa's table.

"How do they look on me?" I asked grandpa.

"You look great," he said, and smiled.

I didn't need new sunglasses. First, the prescription glasses I wore had expensive lenses that automatically turned dark in bright sunlight. Second, I already had a cute pair of sunglasses that I bought before leaving Cambodia. I began wearing sunglasses after observing the wrinkles that had appeared around my eyes.

But when grandpa gave me his sunglasses, I couldn't say no. I knew that giving gifts was one of the last pleasures left to him. He didn't have any money to put into white envelopes anymore—all his retirement payments went directly to the nursing home. So I took grandpa's sunglasses, and slipped them into my purse.

I never wore them.

The Upcoming Birthday

Grandpa's birthday is coming up in a few weeks.

"What do you want for your birthday, grandpa?" I asked one day.

I asked this question and it occurred to me that for as long as I had known him, I had never given grandpa Shlomo a birthday present. But he always gave me gifts. Usually, he gave me money, more cash than I expected.

"What? A birthday present?" he smiled at my question. "I don't need anything. I have everything that I need."

Now that he is so old, maybe the time has come to give him a present, I thought.

How to Communicate Without Words

A reporter from the *Boston Herald* came to interview grandpa Shlomo when he turned one hundred.

The reporter observed that everyone in the nursing home loves grandpa, even though grandpa can't speak English.

How did grandpa Shlomo get to be so popular without speaking?

I am not sure. But I read in the *Herald* that he tried to kiss the reporter's hand when they met for the first time.

The Interview

After grandpa Shlomo turned 100, a *Boston Globe* columnist came to interview him too. The columnist asked if grandpa is angry at the Romanians for what they did to the Jews during the war.

"No," grandpa Shlomo said. "There were some people who were antisemites. They hated the Jews. But not all the Romanians, I am not angry at them."

The reporter then asked my grandpa if he is angry at the Germans for what they did.

"Did I meet them?" grandpa Shlomo replied. "I didn't meet them, so how can I be angry at them?"

The reporter asked grandpa what it's like to be one hundred years old.

Grandpa said it feels great because he has a lot of things to remember.

One Hundred and a Half

I visited grandpa on a winter day after a big snowstorm. It just so happened that it was February 10, so he was exactly one hundred years and six months old. I hadn't seen him in a long time and he looked different, the way people always look different from the way you remember them when it's been a while—especially old people, who always seem to be getting even older. On this day, grandpa Shlomo looked skinnier than he was just a few months ago.

"How much time do you think I have left?" he asked my father tentatively. "I don't feel like I'm dying yet."

"About eight years," my father replied quickly, like he had thought about this before.

I have no idea how he came up with the number eight, but in any case I suppose that eight years must seem like an awfully short time for anyone who is alive, especially someone who has one hundred years behind them. Yet at the same time, it's also an unrealistically long time, because most of the people who are one hundred don't live long enough to turn 101.

But then again, according to statistics (which I just checked), only one in 6,000 people lives to be one hundred, and eighty percent of them are women. So grandpa is good at beating the odds.

Sometimes I kind of catch myself thinking that he might be immortal.

"You should live for another ten years," I told him. "If you do that, you'll beat the national record for men."

"That's not going to be so easy," grandpa protested. "It's one thing if I could work—because I always enjoyed every kind of work—or if I could at least go outside and walk around. But they keep me locked up here all day and I have nothing to do."

Language

One day, when grandpa Shlomo was approaching his 102nd birthday, my father went to visit him as usual, but found that he couldn't communicate with him.

For some reason, on that day, grandpa spoke only in Romanian. My father tried to make him switch to Russian, but grandpa's brain kept going back to the language of his childhood: Romanian. My father does not speak Romanian, and he became terrified that he could not understand what grandpa was saying.

Grandpa Shlomo never spoke Russian perfectly. Even as a child, I remember noticing the grammatical mistakes he made. Russian was not even his second language, but his third or fourth.

Luckily, grandpa's Romanian phase was only temporary. The next time my father came to visit him, grandpa went back to speaking Russian.

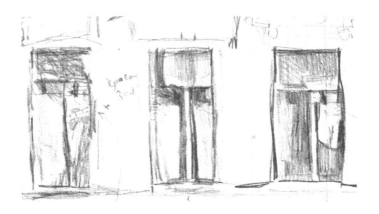

Grandpa's Lost Address Book

After grandpa died, I often overheard my father talking on the phone with aunt Polina. They spent hours remembering the people they used to know, childhood friends, neighbors and relatives. I only heard bits and pieces of what they said, only from my father's side.

"Remember so and so's son? What was his name? Oh, that's right, it must have been that... Did they have two sons? Or a son and a daughter? He must have been a few years younger than me, right? Did they move to Philadelphia? How were they related to us, exactly? It must have been on the father's side... since he used to receive letters from Philadelphia. Oh, remember that uncle? He was the most educated one in our family. They lived in Kyiv. He was the one who encouraged me to go to university. He told me to get a PhD. What became of him?"

And on and on these conversations went.

When grandpa Shlomo died, the connections that he had kept with extended family members became broken. My father only kept in touch with his first cousins, the sons and daughters of grandpa's and grandma's brothers and sisters. But grandpa Shlomo had kept in contact with his cousins, too, and with their children. He must have had their telephone numbers and addresses written down somewhere.

All of the people of his generation had address books, where they recorded, in alphabetical order, the contact information of their friends and family. These handwritten address books stayed with them through life.

"Didn't grandpa have an address book?" I asked my father, after overhearing one of his conversations with aunt Polina, when they were trying to remember the names of their relatives and figure out how to get in touch with them.

"Of course grandpa Shlomo had an address book," my father said.

But it has been lost. Or thrown away in the trash, its value unappreciated.

Ancestors at a Dinner Party

When I was a little girl and my parents first informed me that I am Jewish, they added, "But don't tell anyone!" My mother may have even whispered this warning in a worried voice.

I must have been younger than ten.

I didn't ask them what it meant to be Jewish and why I shouldn't tell anyone. Maybe I thought that I already knew what it meant: It was like being born with a birth defect. It's as if they had said to me, "You only have four toes, but don't tell anyone!"

The first thing I learned about being Jewish is that Jewish people were murdered during the war. It meant that being Jewish was a bad thing, because it made other people hate you. It was like having lice. It's not something you'd be proud of.

Neither in Russia, nor in my family was being Jewish viewed as a religion. It was an ethnicity. If you were born to Jewish parents, your passport would state that you are Jewish. None of us believed in God or kept Jewish customs—besides eating matzah on Passover. We didn't discuss why we ate matzah, it was just something we did because other Jewish people did the same.

Being Jewish was just something you were born with. It was in the curl of the hair, in the shape of the nose. It was important for my parents that we marry someone Jewish, but not for religious reasons. "Jewish husbands don't drink, don't cheat, and don't beat their wives," they'd say. "Jewish parents value education. That's why you should marry someone Jewish."

I don't know of any non-Jewish ancestors on my family tree, although I wish I had some, because I would like to also think of myself as Russian.

With each generation, the number of ancestors increases. From four grandparents, we have eight great-grandparents, and 16 great-great-grandparents. But while I can name all eight of my great-grandparents, I know the names of only eight great-great-grandparents (instead of 16). As for the next generation, I know of only one forefather: Morduch Kaufman, whose birth year was probably in the mid-nineteenth century.

I was thinking that it would be interesting if every baby, upon his or her birth, got a family book: a document with a family tree containing their ancestors' names, places of birth, and years of life. Why don't we do it?

I am imagining a dinner party that never happened, a party where all my ancestors of the same generation could have met each other.

Take for instance my eight great-grandparents, from Russia, Belarus, Ukraine, Romania and Moldova. The genes of these eight people combined together to make me and my brother, yet these individuals who lived about one hundred years ago, had never been to a dinner party together. They were an eye surgeon from Belarus, a doctor from Odessa, an illiterate housewife who sold ice-cream, a hairdresser from Leningrad, and businessmen from Moldova, one of whom owned a shop and sold rugs. I imagine the eight of them at a dinner party one hundred years ago.

"Why are we here?" one would ask, finding himself in a room with strangers.

"We are here because we will be one family in the future," another would reply.

And, I guess, the further that we move forward into the future, the more we can begin to see all of humanity as one family.

Acknowledgements

My father, Alexander Masis, is a gifted storyteller. He has a skill for picking out funny (but true) incidents out of everyday life and turning them into such entertaining stories that everyone who listens to him practically pees their pants laughing. This book was born when I began writing down the stories that my father told at dinnertime—the stories about what grandpa said to him at the nursing home.

This book would not exist without the stories that passed down from grandma and grandpa to my father and my aunt Polina Seltser, and from their brothers and sisters to my father's cousins.

I would like to thank Serghey Daniliuk for driving me to the village of Obodovka, Ukraine, where my grandparents survived World War II, and for telling me about the Russian government's World War II soldiers' database, Pamyat Naroda, which led me to many discoveries.

This book was supplemented with interviews from the USC Visual History Archive that recorded the memories of Holocaust survivors from Ukraine and Moldova in the 1990s. I was able to access the archive through the Jewish Library in Montreal.

A huge thanks to Yelena Lembersky, the author of *Like a Drop of Ink in a Downpour* for inspiring me with her example, for encouraging me to publish the book, and for generously allowing me to use the sketches of her grandfather, Felix Lembersky, as illustrations in this books.

I would also like to thank Alessandra Anzani of Academic Studies Press for recognizing the value in this project.

A huge thank you to my maternal grandfather Simon Belenkiy for encouraging me to write books and for providing the financial support that made the publication of this book possible. My next book will be about him and I already have the title for it: "How my grandfather fell from an airplane."

Finally, I would like to remember Soviet-Jewish author Alexander Raskin, whose collection of short stories *When Daddy Was a Little Boy* (published in 1961) I read when I was growing up. The style and format of his book became the inspiration behind this book.

Sources

1. Testimony of Fira Oussatinski, June 24, 2008, Calgary, Canada, Calgary Jewish Federation, USC Foundation Visual History Archive.
2. Testimony of Oleg Kandel, Aug. 2, 1998, Vyborg, Russia. USC Foundation Visual History Archive.
3. Testimony of Fira Oussatinski. She estimates between 200-300 people were killed in Zguritsa during the pogrom.
4. Testimony of Fira Oussatinski
5. Testimony of Fira Oussatinski
6. Testimony of Freda Rosenblatt. Jan 10, 1995, Ontario, Canada. USC Visual History Archive.
7. Testimony of Petr Roitman, Nov 21, 1995, Israel.

USC Shoah Visual History Archive.
8. Testimony of Petr Roitman
9. Testimony of Petr Roitman
10. Testimony of Faina Chechelnik, June 19, 1995.
    Los Angeles, USA, USC Visual History Archive.
11. Testimony of Raisa Davidovich-Lifshits,
    Sept. 7, 1997. Tel Aviv, Israel. USC Shoah Foundation.
12. Testimony of Beniamin Grinberg, Aug 20, 1997,
    Carmiel, Israel. USC Visual History Archive.
13. Testimony of Petr Roitman
14. Testimony of Iakov Dinovitser, Oct. 6, 1997, Odesa
    Oblast, Ukraine. USC Shoah Visual History Archive.
15. Testimony of Faina Chechelnik
16. Testimony of German Bel'zer, Feb. 23, 1997, Israel.
    USC Shoah Visual History Archive.
17. Testimony of German Bel'zer
18. Testimony of Oleg Kandel
19. Testimony of Fira Oussatinski
20. Testimony of Bronia Alpeeva, Aug. 19, 1997, Drokiia,
    Moldova. USC Shoah Foundation Visual History
    Archive.
21. Interview with Artur Cerari, the Roma Baron of
    Soroca, summer of 2017.
22. Testimony of Rakhil' Aizikova, 1997, Balti,
    Moldova. USC Visual History Archive.
23. Testimony of Petr Roitman

About the Artist

Felix Lembersky (1913-1970) was a Soviet artist. Born in Poland and raised in Ukraine, he practiced art in Kyiv before moving to Leningrad (Saint Petersburg) in the 1930s. He survived the Siege of Leningrad; his parents were murdered by the Nazis in Berdichev, Ukraine. He created images of war and the Holocaust, including "Execution: Babyn Yar" canvases devoted to the massacre of Jews in Kyiv. Drawings in this book come from his sketchbooks, many published for the first time. His work was exhibited internationally and collected by museums in Russia and the U.S.

About the Author

Julie Masis is a freelance journalist, a newspaper publisher and an author. Her stories have been published in the Times of Israel, the Jerusalem Post, the Boston Globe, the Guardian, the Montreal Gazette, the Christian Science Monitor and in other newspapers and magazines. She is also the editor and publisher of the Russian Boston Gazette, a newspaper for the Russian-speaking immigrant community in Boston. She was born in Saint-Petersburg, Russia and immigrated to the United States when she was 10 years old. She has lived in Canada and Cambodia, and reported the news from Ukraine, Moldova, Russia, Vietnam, and other countries.

A note about place names:

When writing about the Second World War and the Soviet period, I used the Russian phonetic spelling of place names in Ukraine and Moldova because that was how those cities were known at the time, and how my grandparents referred to these places when telling stories.

When writing about the modern period, I used the Moldovan and Ukrainian spelling, such as Chisinau and Kiyv (rather than Kishinev and Kiev) because that is how these cities are called nowadays.

However, please keep in mind that Obodovka is the same place as Obodivka (on modern maps), Zguritsa is the same as Zgurita, and Soroki is the same as Soroca.

© Julie Masis 2025

Artwork by Felix Lembersky © Yelena Lembersky